simply ina

A BAREFOOT CONTESSA COOKBOOK

simply ina

BARELY COOKING / SHORTCUT /
MAKE AHEAD / REALLY FAST

ina garten

Photographs by Quentin Bacon

Clarkson Potter / Publishers
NEW YORK

Clarkson Potter/Publishers
An imprint of the Crown Publishing Group
A division of Penguin Random House LLC
1745 Broadway
New York, NY 10019
clarksonpotter.com
penguinrandomhouse.com

Library of Congress Cataloging-in-Publication Data
Names: Garten, Ina author | Bacon, Quentin photographer
Title: Simply Ina: a barefoot Contessa cookbook: barely cooking, shortcut, make ahead, really fast / Ina Garten; photographs by Quentin Bacon.
Description: First edition. | New York: Clarkson Potter/Publishers, [2026] | Includes index.
Identifiers: LCCN 2026009207 (print) LCCN 2026009208 (ebook) | ISBN 9780593234174 hardcover | ISBN 9780593234181 ebook
Subjects: LCSH: Barefoot Contessa (Store) | Cooking | Make-ahead cooking | Quick and easy cooking | LCGFT: Cookbooks
Classification: LCC TX714 .G3646 2026 (print) | LCC TX714 (ebook) | DDC 641.5—dc23/eng/20260318
LC record available at https://lccn.loc.gov/2026009207
LC ebook record available at https://lccn.loc.gov/2026009208

ISBN 978-0-593-23417-4
Costco Edition ISBN 979-8-217-03741-4
Premium Edition
ISBN 979-8-217-03725-4
B&N Premium Edition
ISBN 979-8-217-03726-1
Ebook ISBN 978-0-593-23418-1

Contributing Editor: Pam Krauss
Editor: Jennifer Sit
Editorial assistant: Elaine Hennig
Designer: Marysarah Quinn
Production editor: Terry Deal
Production and prepress color manager: Kim Tyner
Compositor: Merri Ann Morrell
Food stylist: Christine Albano
Prop stylist: Miguel Flores-Vianna
Copy editor: Mark McCauslin
Proofreaders: Rachel Holzman and Rachel Markowitz
Indexer: Elizabeth T. Parson
Publicists: Kate Tyler and Jana Branson
Marketers: Allison Renzulli and Stephanie Davis

Manufactured in China

10 9 8 7 6 5 4 3 2 1

FIRST EDITION

The authorized representative in the EU for product safety and compliance is Penguin Random House Ireland, Morrison Chambers, 32 Nassau Street, Dublin D02 YH68, Ireland, https://eu-contact.penguin.ie.

contents

thank you! 11

intro 13

store-bought is fine 20

drinks & apps 25

lunch 53

dinner 89

sides 129

dessert 165

breakfast & brunch 207

menus 236

resources 246

index 251

recipe index 255

thank you!

The books I write may have my name on them, but they are always a collaboration of wonderful people who work with me. First, thank you to my team: Rose Brown, Mica Bahn, Cindy Massey, and Sarah Chase, who help me, from running my life to running my business, so I can do what I love—write cookbooks. Sarah helps me develop recipes and Rose and Mica work with me to retest them repeatedly until I am sure they will work for you every time you make them.

I've been writing books for Clarkson Potter since 1999 and I'm deeply grateful for all their love and support. My extraordinary editor, Pam Krauss, knows exactly the right words to say to cheer me on and get me past the rough spots. After so many books, creative director Marysarah Quinn still lovingly lets me sit next to her while she designs each page. My dear friends Kate Tyler and Jana Branson on PR send my books out into the world brilliantly. I'm so grateful to the whole team: David Drake, Aaron Wehner, Francis Lam, Jenn Sit, Jill Flaxman, Allison Renzulli, Kim Tyner, and Terry Deal, who oversee the entire publishing process from start to finish.

I also love my photography team. Thank you to Quentin Bacon for the gorgeous photographs, to Christine Albano for the mouthwatering food styling, and to my longtime friend Miguel Flores-Vianna for the style that goes into every photograph. I also want to thank Elizabeth Eichner for allowing us to borrow so much of the beautiful tableware from her store, E-E Home, in Amagansett for this book.

Thank you too to my amazing agent, Esther Newberg, who takes care of business like no one else! And of course, to my sweet husband, Jeffrey, whose constant love and support set me on this wondrous path.

intro

simple not fancy food

It's not easy to make something simple (and delicious).

When I first started cooking, I thought that to be great, food had to be complicated. When I was teaching myself to cook by working my way through Julia Child's *Mastering the Art of French Cooking* I struggled with fancy techniques like "cook in a bain-marie," long prep lists, and recipes with ingredients that were recipes in themselves—I thought surely *those* were the secrets to impressive meals. But after decades of cooking, I've learned something far more important: **the best food is often the simplest.** Truly delicious dishes don't require hours of hands-on time in the kitchen. They just need a little thought and a few good ingredients, preferably in season.

This book is all about **cooking simply,** making the kind of food that fits into your real life. Whether you're making dinner after a long day at work, hosting friends for a cozy weekend supper, or pulling together a last-minute meal because plans changed (and they always do!), **I want you to feel completely confident** that you can cook something delicious without a fuss and it won't just be fine, it will be wonderful.

Simple doesn't necessarily mean you can just slap together a few ingredients and put them on the table, though. It's about cooking with intentionality, investing your time, money, and effort where it counts most so you can focus on the things that really matter, like making your guests feel welcome.

The opposite of cooking simply is what I often see on

social media, with people throwing in one ingredient after another to create BIG flavor. It may seem more sophisticated, but for me, it's just confusing; do all those additions actually make the dish taste better? Good food is a little like a gorgeous dress; if the fabric and the cut are beautiful, it doesn't need a lot of sequins, ruffles, and bows. It just *is* beautiful.

That's why I'm always looking for ways to simplify my cooking. Every recipe in every book goes through the same drill: Does each ingredient earn its place in the recipe? Is the ingredient important enough to the final dish for me to buy it, prep it, and add it? Does it enhance the star ingredient, or does it compete with it? And is there an easier way to create the flavor and texture I'm looking for?

Over the past thirty years that I've been writing cookbooks, I've found many ways to simplify a recipe. I buy best-in-class ingredients that don't need a lot of enhancement to taste amazing. I rely on kitchen tools like a stick blender and a rice cooker that save so much work. And instead of constantly fiddling with something cooking on the stovetop, I put it in the oven, set a timer, and just forget about it.

Each recipe in this book has a secret that makes preparing it easier than you thought. I've labeled them to highlight their superpowers, whether it can be made or prepped ahead; assembled using a good store-bought ingredient; made in a single bowl or pot to make cleanup easy; or cooked really, really quickly. Some are so easy I've actually labeled them "barely cooking"! In a world where everyone is overbooked, overstressed, and communicating via screens all day rather than in person, connecting around a beautifully set table with delicious, simple food can be the most healing thing you can do for the people you love.

Some recipes in this book come together especially quickly with little or no time spent at the stove. My Cheddar & Chive Omelet (page 80) has a short ingredient list and cooks in just minutes. The Roasted Halibut with Potato Chip Crust (page 119), which looks and tastes more like a restaurant meal, goes from pantry to table in less than half an hour. And if you don't consider toasting bread cooking, my Fig, Blue Cheese & Prosciutto Tartines (page 68) and Strawberries Romanoff (page 172) don't require any cooking at all!

In other cases, I rely on prepared products from the grocery store, like pasta sauce or mashed potatoes, to jump-start a recipe. (There really *are* times when I think that "store-bought is just fine.") When I do, though, I often use them as an ingredient, not as a final product. For example, when I add slowly cooked garlic, half-and-half, and lots of seasoning to store-bought prepared mashed potatoes, they taste like they were made from scratch—and I haven't peeled a single potato!

My Cabbage & Sprout Slaw (page 160) starts with a bag of shredded coleslaw mix plus a bag of shredded Brussels sprouts, so not only do you not have to cut up the veggies, you aren't left with half a cabbage knocking around in your refrigerator drawer. And because the recipe is made in one bowl, you don't end up with a sink full of dishes and graters, either. Roast Duck Legs with Cherry Sauce (page 105) starts with cooked confit duck legs that I order online and keep in the freezer. All I need to do is reheat the duck so the skin is nice and crispy, and I make a sauce with basically three ingredients—mustard, red currant jelly, and dried cherries. Voilà! Dinner is served.

I even figured out how this would work for dessert. My Raspberry Cheesecake (page 194) starts with a cheesecake from a bakery that I top with fresh raspberries and a shortcut raspberry sauce that is thickened with a jar of good jam! No need to spend anxious minutes staring at the oven door wondering whether the cheesecake is done so it doesn't crater in the middle when it cools!

I should add that using store-bought shortcuts isn't a universal silver bullet. There were a lot of dishes that didn't make the cut. Baking mixes always taste like baking mixes; their texture and flavor cannot be masked even by adding good chocolate and pure vanilla extract to the batter. I tried all the brands of mashed potatoes, from boxed flakes to refrigerated prepared potatoes, to find the brand that has the best flavor. I did the experimenting so you don't have to, and you'll find my choices right there in the recipes. It wasn't always easy, but it was so much fun to test them all. I've listed some of my favorite store-bought ingredients on page 20 so you can keep your fridge and pantry stocked just like I do.

The recipes that I find myself using over and over again are those you can make entirely ahead of time, or that can be prepped and assembled in advance, then finished right before serving. And that is actually **the secret to a great dinner party**—when the hosts are having as much fun as the guests.

hot-rodding

Making large batches of a recipe to eat for days is *not* one of my tricks for simplifying mealtime. Frankly, I'm not crazy about leftovers. There are many times when I'll cook something totally delicious and enjoy it for dinner, but even though there is enough left to serve it again, I really don't look forward to eating it the next night—it's never as good as it was the first time!

However, **there's another way to think about leftovers.** Why not consider them "precooked" ingredients? Leftover Caramelized Butternut Squash & Cranberries (page 140), once it's been cooled, refrigerated, and reheated, loses a lot of the texture and flavor that made it delicious hot out of the oven. But that doesn't mean you can't turn it into something else. You can add some sautéed onions, apple cider, and seasonings, and purée it to make Easy Butternut Squash & Apple Soup (page 57). Or toss it into Charlie Bird's Autumn Salad (page 75), so fresh ingredients like arugula, farro, and Parmesan cheese and the vinaigrette wake up the butternut squash in a whole new way.

This is what I affectionately call "hot-rodding." It's like a car souped up with extra parts to make it go faster. I do the same thing with the prepared foods I buy. Think about it: A specialty food store prepares a pasta pesto salad. They put it in the refrigerated case, you take it home and refrigerate it again, and maybe serve it the next day. It's already leftovers!

So, before I serve prepared foods, I hot-rod them. The pasta pesto that I bought? I add salt and pepper because their flavors will have diminished. If I have some pesto in the fridge and peas in the freezer, I'll add them too, plus lots of freshly grated Parmesan cheese, for a delicious pasta pesto and pea salad. If I bring home Italian wedding soup from a store, I'll add some of my homemade chicken stock to give it more flavor and then check the seasonings. I don't think there is a dish that can't be improved by a little edge from freshly squeezed lemon juice, a splash of good vinegar, or some grated Parmesan cheese, whether it's takeout or something from your own refrigerator shelf.

I've tested every recipe in this book over and over again to make sure it's simple, satisfying, and completely doable. I want you to be able to make food that brings people together—the kind that makes your friends linger at the table just a little longer. **Because simple food shouldn't just save you time; it should let you enjoy the people you love.**

So, pour yourself a glass of wine, turn on some good music, and share a simple meal with friends. You'll be so glad you did!

xxxx Ina

Truffle butter

Marinara sauce

Marinated cheese

Mayonnaise

Nutella

Frozen puff pastry

store-bought is fine

Frozen peas

Duck legs confit

Baked beans

Caramel sauce

Granola

Meringues

KitchenAid
Turntable Microwave Oven

OLIO SANTO
CALIFORNIA
OLIVE OIL
EXTRA VIRGIN
OLIVE
OIL

drinks & apps

watermelon lemonade

frozen piña coladas

classic cosmopolitans

caipiroska

sparkling rhubarb

roasted shrimp
with lemon caper mayonnaise

herbed goat cheese spread

salmon rillettes

emergency blue cheese dip

whipped ricotta
with fig jam & grilled bread

mediterranean mezze board

12 no-cook appetizers

principles of hosting

A friend once told me that she thinks the best part of a party is actually the invitation; how funny is that? But when I thought about it, I realized that she's right. Being invited to someone's home says, "You matter to me. I want to spend the evening with you."

That's why for me, the most important part of hosting might be how you make your guests feel when they arrive. When I asked my friend Frank Bruni, a journalist, columnist, and former restaurant critic for *The New York Times*, what's the most critical thing in the success of a restaurant, he said, "How you're greeted at the door." Wow—the food and the setting are secondary? It's the same thing at a dinner party. People may not remember what you served for dinner, but they will remember how they felt at your house, and how they're welcomed sets up the whole evening.

When I have a party, I don't just leave the door open so people can let themselves in; I like to greet each person individually. I want good smells to be wafting from the kitchen, fun music playing, and delicious cocktails and nibbles on the long table in the living room so I can make sure everyone has a drink without my leaving the room. This is where a simple dinner makes a difference; if most of the preparation is done before guests arrive, all I need is a timer to tell me when the Easy Lobster Bake (page 115) or Baked Croque Monsieurs (page 79) need to come out of the oven.

The next time you entertain, instead of stressing, fix yourself a cocktail and greet your friends at the door as though you don't have a care in the world because you know you've got a delicious dinner waiting for everyone.

watermelon lemonade

MAKES 6 TO 8 (8-OUNCE) DRINKS

This summer drink is inspired by one in my friend Sarah Chase's New England Open-House Cookbook. *Somehow the strawberries make the watermelon taste better, even though you don't know they're in the mixture. Make a large pitcher because you won't be able to stop drinking it!*

- 3 cups (1-inch) diced seedless red watermelon, lightly packed
- ¾ cup fresh strawberries, hulled and diced (4 medium)
- ½ cup freshly squeezed lemon juice (2 to 3 lemons)
- ½ cup superfine sugar
- 3 cups bottled or tap water
- Ice cubes, lemon slices, and mint sprigs, for serving

Place the watermelon, strawberries, lemon juice, sugar, and ½ cup of the bottled water in a high-speed blender, such as Vitamix. Purée for one full minute. Place a large mesh strainer over a bowl and pour the mixture through the strainer, discarding the solids. Pour into a pitcher and add the remaining 2½ cups of water.

Fill 8-ounce glasses halfway with ice, pour in the lemonade mixture, and garnish with lemon and mint. Serve ice cold.

If you only have a traditional blender, it may take longer to strain the purée, as it will be a bit coarser.

frozen piña coladas

MAKES 4 (8-OUNCE) DRINKS

If you don't count toasting the coconut, this is a no-cook recipe. Of course, you can use any rum you like, but I prefer the complex flavor of dark rum, and golden pineapple tends to be sweeter than traditional ones, if you can find one.

- 1 cup sweetened shredded coconut
- 2 cups (large-diced) fresh pineapple, preferably golden, peeled and cored
- 3 cups ice cubes
- 1 cup Coco López cream of coconut, well mixed
- 1 cup dark rum, preferably Cruzan
- ½ cup frozen diced mango
- 3 tablespoons freshly squeezed lime juice (2 to 3 limes)
- Pineapple wedges, for serving

Place the coconut in a medium (10-inch) dry sauté pan over medium-low heat and cook for 8 to 12 minutes, tossing frequently, until evenly golden brown. Set aside to cool to room temperature.

Meanwhile, place the diced pineapple, ice, cream of coconut, rum, mango, and lime juice in a blender. Add ½ cup of the toasted coconut (reserve the rest for garnishing the drinks). Blend on medium speed for about one minute until totally smooth.

Pour into glasses and garnish with a sprinkle of toasted coconut and a pineapple wedge. Serve ice cold.

NO COOKING

classic cosmopolitans

MAKES 6 DRINKS

During the pandemic, I made a very large Cosmopolitan on Instagram that turned out to be just what we all needed at that moment. For the perfect Cosmo, there are two important ingredients: cranberry juice cocktail (not pure cranberry juice) and freshly squeezed lime juice.

2 cups (16 ounces) good vodka
1 cup (8 ounces) Cointreau or triple sec
1 cup (8 ounces) Ocean Spray cranberry juice cocktail
½ cup freshly squeezed lime juice (4 limes)

Place martini or coupe glasses in the freezer for at least 15 minutes.

Pour the vodka, Cointreau, cranberry juice cocktail, and lime juice into a pitcher. Fill a cocktail shaker half full with ice. Pour the drink mixture into the cocktail shaker until it's three-quarters full, cover with the lid, and shake for a full 30 seconds (it's longer than you think!). Strain the mixture into the frozen glasses and serve ice cold. Repeat with the remaining drink mixture.

caipiroska

MAKES ONE DRINK

On the beach in Montauk there is a wonderful restaurant called Mostrador Marram, an offshoot of the restaurant Mostrador in Uruguay. They make this classic drink that tastes like the most refreshing limeade but it's actually a cocktail. I love it so much, I bought a little machine that makes shaved ice, but you could also use small ice cubes.

Ice, preferably shaved or small cubes
2 ounces freshly squeezed lime juice (2 limes)
2 ounces good vodka
1 ounce simple syrup (see note)
2 lime quarters

For simple syrup, combine 1 cup sugar with 1 cup water in a small pot and heat just until the sugar dissolves. Refrigerate until cold.

Fill an 8-ounce highball glass with the ice and set aside.

Pour the lime juice, vodka, and simple syrup into a cocktail shaker. Squeeze the juice from the lime quarters into the shaker and add the squeezed rinds to the shaker, too. Add the ice from the glass and shake for at least 30 seconds (it's longer than you think!). Pour the entire contents of the shaker (including the ice and lime rinds) into the glass and serve ice cold.

MAKE AHEAD

sparkling rhubarb

MAKES 6 TO 8 DRINKS

Jeffrey and I went to a fantastic museum outside Copenhagen called Louisiana Museum of Modern Art. This surprising drink was on the menu in the café; I had to make it when I got home! The tartness of the fresh rhubarb is balanced with sugar and vanilla. It's so refreshing!

8 cups (1-inch) diced fresh rhubarb (about 2 pounds)
1 cup sugar
½ teaspoon pure vanilla extract
Ice cubes, for serving
Cold sparkling water, such as San Pellegrino

Combine the rhubarb, sugar, and 4 cups water in a large pot. Bring to a boil, lower the heat, and simmer for 15 minutes. Remove from the heat. Add the vanilla and strain the mixture into a bowl, pressing lightly on the rhubarb. Discard the solids. Cover the syrup tightly and chill.

Fill glasses one-quarter full with the rhubarb syrup. Add a few ice cubes then fill with the sparkling water. Serve ice cold.

MAKE AHEAD

roasted shrimp
with lemon caper mayonnaise

SERVES 6

Once you've roasted shrimp instead of boiling them in water, you'll never go back; they have so much more flavor and can be served warm or at room temperature. This sauce with fresh chives, lemon, capers, and mustard comes together in a minute and lasts for days in the fridge.

1 cup good mayonnaise, such as Hellmann's
2 tablespoons minced fresh chives, plus extra for serving
1½ teaspoons grated lemon zest
1½ tablespoons freshly squeezed lemon juice
1½ tablespoons brine-packed capers, rinsed, drained, and minced
2 teaspoons good Dijon mustard, such as Grey Poupon
Kosher salt and freshly ground black pepper
1½ pounds (16 to 20-count) shrimp, peeled and deveined with tails on
Good olive oil
Kosher salt and freshly ground black pepper

In a medium bowl, whisk together the mayonnaise, chives, lemon zest, lemon juice, capers, mustard, 1 teaspoon salt, and ¼ teaspoon pepper. Cover and chill until ready to serve. (The sauce can be refrigerated for up to 3 days.)

Preheat the oven to 400 degrees.

Dry the shrimp with paper towels. Place the shrimp on a sheet pan and toss them with 3 tablespoons olive oil, 1½ teaspoons salt, and ¾ teaspoon pepper. Spread in a single layer and roast for 7 minutes, until just firm and pink.

Spoon the mayonnaise into a small bowl and place on a platter. Sprinkle the sauce with chives and surround it with the shrimp.

SHORTCUT

herbed goat cheese spread

MAKES ¾ CUP

My friend Lori Chemla, who co-owns Carissa's Bakery in East Hampton, makes this incredibly easy appetizer. I'm a big fan of the delicious marinated sheep & goat cheese from Meredith Dairy. It comes in a jar with herbed oil and you'll find it in the refrigerated section of your grocery store. It's creamy and tangy and needs very little to make it into a delicious spread to put on toasts.

1 (11.2-ounce) jar Meredith Dairy marinated sheep & goat cheese

½ teaspoon minced fresh thyme leaves plus 1 sprig fresh thyme

Kosher salt and freshly ground black pepper

6 to 8 slices country bread, grilled or toasted and cut into pieces

Drain the cheese, reserving the oil and discarding the thyme sprig and peppercorns from the jar. Place the cheese in the bowl of a food processor fitted with the steel blade and add 1 teaspoon of the reserved oil, the minced thyme, ⅛ teaspoon salt, and ⅛ teaspoon pepper. Pulse just until smooth.

Transfer the mixture to a small bowl, and top with the fresh thyme sprig and a drizzle of the reserved oil. Serve cold or at room temperature with the bread.

MAKE AHEAD

salmon rillettes

SERVES 6

Eric Ripert is the brilliant and charming co-owner of Le Bernardin in NYC. This recipe that combines both smoked and poached salmon is adapted from the recipe in his gorgeous cookbook Seafood Simple. *Poaching the salmon in white wine and shallots for just 2 or 3 minutes and folding those shallots into the mixture gives this spread layers of flavor.*

2 cups dry white wine, such as Chablis
1 tablespoon minced shallots
1 pound raw salmon fillet, skin and bones removed, 1-inch diced
3 ounces thinly sliced smoked salmon, such as Scottish or Norwegian, chopped
½ cup good mayonnaise, such as Hellmann's
3 tablespoons freshly squeezed lemon juice
Kosher salt and freshly ground black pepper
2 tablespoons minced fresh chives, plus extra for serving
1 baguette sliced ¼-inch thick, toasted

In a large (12-inch) sauté pan, bring the wine, shallots, and 2 cups water to a boil. Lower the heat to a simmer and add the raw salmon. Return to a simmer and cook for 2 to 3 minutes, until the salmon is just opaque, turning any pieces that aren't fully immersed.

With a slotted spoon, transfer the salmon to a plate lined with paper towels. Pour the poaching liquid through a strainer, discarding the liquid. Place the shallots in a medium bowl along with the poached salmon. Refrigerate uncovered for 30 minutes.

Add the smoked salmon, mayonnaise, and lemon juice to the salmon mixture and combine gently, breaking up the poached salmon until it's flaked. Add 1 teaspoon salt and ½ teaspoon pepper, taste for seasonings, and chill. Just before serving, stir in the chives and spoon into a small bowl. Sprinkle with salt and extra chives and serve with the toasted baguette.

emergency blue cheese dip

MAKES 1½ CUPS

For last-minute guests, this dip can be made with ingredients you probably already have in the fridge, and it literally takes only five minutes to prepare. The sweetness of the sherry vinegar balances the sharpness of the Roquefort perfectly.

6 ounces Roquefort cheese, at room temperature
3 ounces cream cheese, at room temperature
2/3 cup good mayonnaise, such as Hellmann's
1½ tablespoons sherry vinegar
Kosher salt and freshly ground black pepper
Crudités, such as celery, carrots, snap peas, and radishes, for serving

Place the Roquefort in the bowl of a food processor fitted with the steel blade. Add the cream cheese, mayonnaise, vinegar, 1 teaspoon salt, and ½ teaspoon pepper and purée until smooth, scraping down the bowl as needed. Transfer to a serving bowl and serve with the crudités.

MAKE AHEAD: *Prepare the dip a few days in advance, cover, and refrigerate. Prep the vegetables, place in a plastic bag with a damp paper towel or an ice cube, and refrigerate.*

whipped ricotta
with fig jam & grilled bread

SERVES 6

You will be amazed how good fig jam and ricotta taste together! This delicious appetizer can be served two ways—you can assemble the toasts or just put out bowls of whipped ricotta and fig jam and let everyone help themselves.

3 cups fresh ricotta (24 ounces)
¼ teaspoon crushed red pepper flakes
Kosher salt and freshly ground black pepper
¼ cup mild olive oil
Good fig jam
6 large (½-inch-thick) slices country bread, grilled or toasted

Place the ricotta, red pepper flakes, 2 teaspoons salt, and ½ teaspoon black pepper in the bowl of a food processor fitted with the steel blade. Pulse six times. With the food processor running, slowly pour the oil down the feed tube and process for about 30 seconds, just until the mixture is thick and smooth.

Transfer the ricotta mixture to a bowl, spoon the fig jam into a second bowl, and serve with grilled bread.

ASSEMBLED

mediterranean mezze board

I love to collect delicious ingredients and arrange them beautifully on a board. For these Mediterranean appetizers, I garnished the store-bought hummus with toasted pine nuts and the baba ganoush with pomegranate arils. They're beautiful and delicious and no one needs to know you didn't make everything yourself.

Fresh fig leaves, if available
Hummus, store-bought
Pine nuts, toasted
Good olive oil
Baba ganoush, store-bought
Pomegranate arils
Block of Greek feta cheese, thickly sliced
Dried herbes de Provence, preferably without lavender
Hothouse cucumbers, cut into slices or spears
Stuffed grape leaves, store-bought
Cherry tomatoes on the vine
Fresh figs, if available
Mixed Greek olives
Whole grain bread, toasted and cut into shards
Pita bread, toasted and cut into triangles

On a large board, arrange the fig leaves (if using) in a single layer. Place two small bowls on the board. Spoon the hummus into one bowl, sprinkle it with the pine nuts, and drizzle with olive oil. Spoon the baba ganoush into the second bowl, sprinkle it with pomegranate arils, and drizzle with olive oil. Lay the feta on the board, sprinkle it with the herbes de Provence, and drizzle it with olive oil.

Lay the cucumbers, stuffed grape leaves, cherry tomatoes, figs (if using), olives, toasted bread, and pita on the board in an artful way. Serve the mezze board at room temperature with serving knives and small plates.

Guacamole

Tortilla chips

Radishes with butter and salt

Tzatziki and pita triangles

Roasted, salted cashews

Cheese straws

12 no-cook appetizers

Sliced salami

Baba ganoush
with pomegranate arils

Terra Chips

Figs with blue cheese

Good olives

Italian Parmesan shards

lunch

easy butternut squash & apple soup

frico crisps

tortellini in brodo

homemade chicken stock

mashed potato & leek soup

tomato parmesan toasts

fig, blue cheese & prosciutto tartines

truffled egg salad

waldorf salad

charlie bird's autumn salad

frisée aux lardons

baked croque monsieurs

cheddar & chive omelet

endive & avocado salad

roasted cauliflower salad

real greek salad

the perfect omelet

Sometimes the simplest things can be the hardest to execute. An omelet is the perfect example. It's basically just three eggs and some filling but it's not so easy to make a great one. I've told this story before—when Jeffrey and I were first married, I invited twenty people for brunch and decided to make each person an omelet. It was a disaster! First, I'm not even sure I really knew how to make a good omelet. More importantly, making twenty omelets meant I was in the kitchen the whole time, and one person can't possibly make twenty hot omelets all at once. Lesson learned!

Many years later, I decided to spend a week perfecting that dish, and the recipe for a Gruyère Omelet ended up in my book *Go-To Dinners*. It's a delicious main course for lunch or brunch, and you probably already have the ingredients in the fridge. It's also a very inexpensive yet elegant meal, and once

you get the technique down, it's really easy. That said, it does take a bit of practice to get it just right.

Soon after that book was published, I was filming my show *Be My Guest*. I asked my guest what we should cook together, and he said he'd love to learn how to make a great omelet. I thought my omelet skills had gotten better but still had a way to go. So, I researched everything I could find about how to make an omelet and came across a video of Jacques Pépin, the ultimate French chef, making one. He did three simple things that I'd never thought of doing when I was making an omelet and they took my omelet skills from "perfectly fine" to "great"! The Cheddar & Chive Omelet on page 80 is the result and now you too will be able to make a true French omelet that you'd be proud to serve to anyone, even Jacques Pépin.

SHORTCUT

easy butternut squash & apple soup

SERVES 4

I've made butternut squash soup before, but this is equally delicious and much easier to make because you start with precut squash and use a stick blender to purée it right in the pot. Perfect autumn lunch; no stress!

Good olive oil
2 cups chopped yellow onions (2 onions)
2 pounds precut butternut squash
1 pound sweet apples, such as Gala, peeled, cored, and diced (2 to 3 apples)
Kosher salt and freshly ground black pepper
1½ cups fresh apple cider, plus extra, if needed
4 Frico Crisps (page 58), optional

Heat 3 tablespoons olive oil in a medium (11-inch) Dutch oven, such as Le Creuset, over medium-low heat. Add the onions and sauté for 5 to 10 minutes, until the onions are tender but not browned, stirring occasionally.

Add the squash, apples, 1 teaspoon salt, ½ teaspoon pepper, and 1 cup water to the pot. Bring to a boil, lower the heat, cover, and simmer for 35 to 40 minutes, until the squash and apples are very soft. Add the apple cider and purée with a stick blender. (You can also use a regular blender.) If the soup is too thick, add a little more apple cider. Add one more teaspoon of salt, check the seasonings, and serve hot with frico crisps (if using).

frico crisps

This is the ultimate one-ingredient recipe. You place tablespoons of grated Italian Parmesan cheese on a sheet pan lined with parchment paper and put them in the oven. In less than 10 minutes, you've got a great crisp snack or crouton for soup.

Grated (ground) Italian Parmesan cheese (see note)

Preheat the oven to 375 degrees.

Line a sheet pan with parchment paper. For each frico, place grated Parmesan in small piles, 2 tablespoons each, on the paper, allowing some space between each pile. Bake for 5 to 8 minutes, until browned. Set aside on the sheet pan; they will crisp as they cool.

Although I always refer to it as "grated" Parmesan, it's actually ground, not grated. I just small-dice a wedge of Italian Parmesan and grind it in the bowl of a food processor fitted with the steel blade until finely ground.

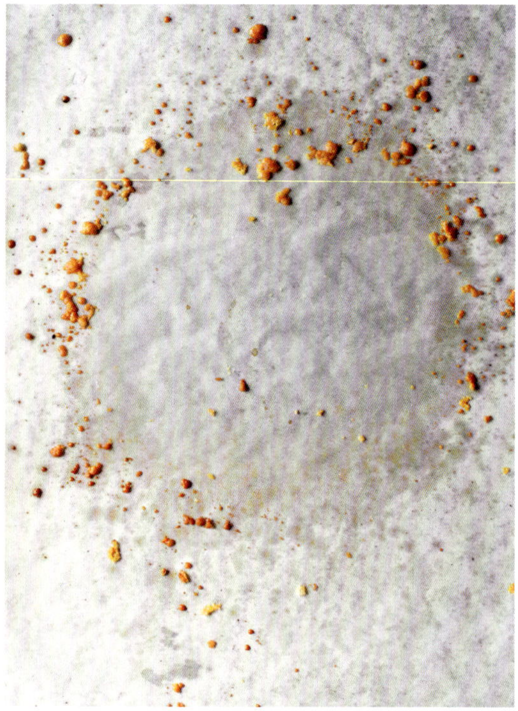

SHORTCUT

tortellini in brodo

SERVES 8

There really is no substitute for homemade chicken stock that simmers for hours on the stove. Once you have a batch in the freezer, you can make this soup in a snap. If you freeze the finished soup, the tortellini will absorb a lot of the stock, so just add some water or more stock when you reheat it.

Good olive oil
2 cups chopped yellow onions (2 onions)
2 cups chopped leeks, white and light green parts (1 large), washed and spun dry
2 cups medium-diced carrots (3 to 5 carrots)
2 cups medium-diced celery (4 large stalks)
12 cups simmering chicken stock, preferably homemade (page 63)
Kosher salt and freshly ground black pepper
1 pound fresh or defrosted cheese tortellini
2 chicken breasts from a rotisserie chicken, skin removed, diced
¼ cup minced fresh parsley

Chicken stock keeps for 6 months in the freezer.

Heat 3 tablespoons olive oil in a large (12 to 13-inch) Dutch oven, such as Le Creuset, over medium heat. Add the onions, leeks, carrots, and celery and sauté for 10 minutes, stirring occasionally. Add the chicken stock, 2 teaspoons salt, and 1 teaspoon pepper and bring to a boil.

Add the tortellini, bring to a simmer, and cook for 8 to 10 minutes, or according to package instructions. Stir in the chicken, bring back to a simmer, then sprinkle with parsley and serve in shallow bowls.

MAKE AHEAD

homemade chicken stock

MAKES 5 TO 6 QUARTS

I am never without quarts of good chicken stock in the freezer; I use it for soups, sauces, and just plain when I need a satisfying warm drink. If you haven't made it before, you'll see that it takes very little time and just bubbles away on the stove while you putter around the house.

3 (5-pound) roasting chickens
3 large yellow onions, unpeeled and quartered
6 carrots, scrubbed and halved
4 celery stalks with leaves, cut in thirds
4 parsnips, scrubbed and halved
20 sprigs fresh parsley
15 sprigs fresh thyme
20 sprigs fresh dill
1 head garlic, unpeeled and cut in half crosswise
2 tablespoons kosher salt
2 teaspoons whole black peppercorns

Place the chickens, onions, carrots, celery, parsnips, parsley, thyme, dill, garlic, salt, and peppercorns in a 16 to 20-quart stockpot. Add 7 quarts of water and bring to a boil. Lower the heat and simmer uncovered for 4 hours.

Cool the stock slightly, strain the entire contents of the pot through a colander into a large bowl or pot, and pack in quart or pint containers, discarding the solids. Refrigerate for up to 4 days or freeze for up to 6 months.

SHORTCUT

mashed potato & leek soup

SERVES 6 TO 8

There are several brands of mashed potatoes in the supermarket, but I think Bob Evans has the best flavor and texture. This potato leek soup is so delicious that no one will guess that you "cheated" a little. (Your secret is safe with me.) However, homemade chicken stock, which you can make ahead and store in the freezer, makes all the difference.

Good olive oil
2 tablespoons unsalted butter
6 cups chopped leeks, white and light green parts (3 to 4 leeks), washed and spun dry
4 cups good chicken stock, preferably homemade (page 63)
2 (24-ounce) packages Bob Evans original mashed potatoes
4 tablespoons dry white wine, such as Pinot Grigio, divided (see note)
2 teaspoons minced fresh thyme leaves
Kosher salt and freshly ground black pepper
Minced fresh chives, for serving

Heat 2 tablespoons olive oil and the butter in a large pot or medium (10 to 11-inch) Dutch oven, such as Le Creuset. Add the leeks and cook over medium to medium-high heat for 8 to 10 minutes, stirring occasionally, until the leeks are tender but not browned.

Add the chicken stock, mashed potatoes, 2 tablespoons of the wine, the thyme, 1 tablespoon salt, and 2 teaspoons pepper. Bring to a boil, lower the heat, and simmer for 10 minutes, stirring occasionally to break up the potatoes. Purée with a stick blender (you can also use a regular blender), add the remaining 2 tablespoons of wine, and taste for seasonings. Serve hot, sprinkled with minced chives.

If you don't want to use wine, you can just leave it out.

SHORTCUT

tomato parmesan toasts

SERVES 4

When tomatoes are in season at the local farm stands, I'm always looking for more ways to use them. Cookbook writer Ali Slagle published a recipe in The New York Times *that inspired this delicious sandwich. Prepared pesto is a great shortcut for the Parmesan pesto mayonnaise that you slather on the toast.*

½ cup good mayonnaise, such as Hellmann's
½ cup freshly grated Italian Parmesan cheese
2 tablespoons store-bought pesto, or more to taste
Kosher salt and freshly ground black pepper
3 small, ripe heirloom tomatoes
4 large slices from a country or sourdough loaf
Julienned fresh basil leaves

In a small bowl, stir together the mayonnaise, Parmesan, pesto, and ¼ teaspoon salt. Core the tomatoes and slice them crosswise in ½-inch-thick slices. Toast the bread until lightly browned.

Place the warm bread on a board and slather the slices thickly with the mayonnaise mixture. Arrange the tomato slices on top in a single layer, sprinkle generously with salt, pepper, and the basil, and serve while the toast is warm.

fig, blue cheese & prosciutto tartines

SERVES 4

I had a basket of ripe figs in the refrigerator and wanted to make some tartines for lunch, so I decided on this classic combination. I love the crisp bread with creamy blue cheese, sweet figs, and salty prosciutto. A drizzle of honey and some flake salt make it irresistible!

4 large slices from a country or sourdough loaf
8 ounces Roquefort or Maytag blue cheese, at room temperature
12 tablespoons (1½ sticks) unsalted butter, at room temperature
6 large or 12 small ripe figs, stems removed, sliced (¼-inch thick) lengthwise
8 slices Italian prosciutto di Parma
Good runny honey
Flake sea salt, such as Maldon

Lightly toast the bread in a toaster and place the four slices on a cutting board.

Place the blue cheese and butter in a small bowl and mash them together with a fork. Spread the mixture thickly on the toasted bread.

Arrange overlapping slices of figs on the cheese mixture, then place 2 ribbons of prosciutto down the middle. Drizzle with honey, sprinkle with sea salt, and serve at room temperature.

SHORTCUT

truffled egg salad

MAKES 2½ CUPS

The cookbook writer Sarah Chase is one of my cooking gurus. I love her style of simple, fresh food. This egg salad is from her wonderful New England Open-House Cookbook. *Eggs with truffle butter appeals to my love of high/low food, like potato chips with caviar, so I always have some truffle butter in the freezer!*

9 hard-boiled eggs, peeled, store-bought or homemade (see note, page 220)

1½ tablespoons white truffle butter, such as Urbani, at room temperature

⅓ cup good mayonnaise, such as Hellmann's

2 tablespoons minced fresh chives or scallions (white and green parts)

Kosher salt and freshly ground black pepper

4 slices from a ciabatta or whole grain loaf (optional)

Remove the yolks from two of the eggs and place them on a small plate; reserve the whites. Add the truffle butter and mash them together with a fork.

Place the two reserved egg whites and the rest of the eggs in the bowl of a food processor fitted with the steel blade and pulse a few times *just* until they are very coarsely chopped. (You can also chop them with a knife.) Add the yolk mixture, mayonnaise, chives, 1 teaspoon salt, and ½ teaspoon pepper and pulse a few times just to combine. Taste for seasonings and serve in a sandwich or on its own.

waldorf salad

SERVES 4 FOR LUNCH / 6 AS A SIDE DISH

This is an old-fashioned salad, updated. This recipe is inspired by one created by my friend Erin French in her fabulous book The Lost Kitchen. *I love that she uses fennel, Cheddar, and caramelized pecans in addition to the classic ingredients.*

2 large Honeycrisp or other crisp red apples, unpeeled and ½-inch diced

Small fennel bulb, halved, cored, and thinly sliced crosswise, fronds reserved

4 tender inner celery stalks, sliced ½ inch thick crosswise, leaves reserved

Grated zest and juice of 1 large navel orange

⅓ cup good mayonnaise, such as Hellmann's

2 tablespoons runny honey

Kosher salt and freshly ground black pepper

½ cup golden raisins

6 ounces sharp white Cheddar, such as Cabot, ½-inch diced

½ cup whole fresh flat-leaf parsley leaves

½ cup store-bought caramelized or candied pecans

Combine the apples, fennel, celery, orange zest, and orange juice in a large bowl. Stir in the mayonnaise, honey, 2½ teaspoons salt, and 1 teaspoon pepper. Stir in the raisins, Cheddar, and parsley. Just before serving, stir in the pecans, taste for seasonings, and garnish with the fennel fronds and celery leaves. Serve cold or at room temperature.

PREP AHEAD

charlie bird's autumn salad

SERVES 4 FOR LUNCH / 6 AS A SIDE DISH

One of the recipes I've made the most is the Charlie Bird Farro Salad from my book Cook Like a Pro. Recently I met Ryan Hardy, the owner of Charlie Bird restaurant and the creator of this amazing salad. He told me that he makes different seasonal variations all year long, so I came up with this version with butternut squash.

- 4 cups (¾-inch) precut butternut squash (1 pound)
- 3 tablespoons plus ¾ cup good olive oil, divided
- Kosher salt and freshly ground black pepper
- 1 cup pearled farro (6 ounces)
- 1 cup fresh apple cider
- 2 bay leaves
- ½ cup freshly squeezed lemon juice (2 to 3 lemons)
- ½ cup roasted, salted pistachios, coarsely chopped
- 1 cup coarsely chopped fresh parsley
- 1 cup coarsely chopped mint leaves (2 bunches)
- 1 cup cherry or grape tomatoes, halved through the stem
- ⅓ cup thinly sliced radishes (2 to 3 radishes)
- 2 cups baby arugula (2 to 3 ounces)
- ½ cup shaved Italian Parmesan cheese

Preheat the oven to 425 degrees. Place the squash on a sheet pan, toss with the 3 tablespoons olive oil, 1½ teaspoons salt, and ¾ teaspoon pepper, and roast for 20 minutes, tossing occasionally, until browned and tender.

Meanwhile, place the farro, apple cider, bay leaves, 2 teaspoons salt, and 2 cups water in a medium saucepan. Bring to a boil, lower the heat, and simmer uncovered for about 30 minutes, until the farro is tender. (If the liquid evaporates before the farro is tender, add a little more water.) Drain the farro and transfer to a large serving bowl. Discard the bay leaves.

Meanwhile, in a 2-cup glass measuring cup, whisk together the ¾ cup olive oil, the lemon juice, 1½ teaspoons salt, and ¾ teaspoon pepper. Stir ½ of the vinaigrette into the warm farro and set aside for at least 15 minutes to cool.

Before serving, stir the pistachios, parsley, mint, tomatoes, and radishes into the farro. Add the arugula, squash, and the remaining vinaigrette and lightly fold in the Parmesan so as not to break it up too much. Sprinkle with salt and serve.

PREP AHEAD

frisée aux lardons

SERVES 4

No one makes a better frisée aux lardons than the restaurant Balthazar in NYC. This salad was inspired by their recipe; you can prep the croutons, bacon, shallots, and frisée early in the day and cook the dressing at the last minute so the cold lettuce is crisp when you pour on the hot bacon dressing. Who wouldn't love that?

¾ cup good olive oil, divided
6 cups (1-inch) diced white bread cubes from a country loaf (crusts removed)
Kosher salt and freshly ground black pepper
½ pound (½-inch-thick) sliced slab bacon, cut into ½-inch julienne
½ cup thinly sliced shallots (2 large)
½ cup good sherry vinegar
¾ to 1 pound frisée lettuce
4 Jammy Eggs

Heat ½ cup of the olive oil in a large (12-inch) sauté pan over medium-high heat until hot. Add the bread and sprinkle generously with salt and pepper. Cook for 5 to 6 minutes, tossing often, until evenly browned. Transfer to a plate. (Don't wipe out the pan.)

Add the bacon to the pan and cook over medium-high heat for 5 to 7 minutes, tossing often, until evenly browned. (Don't pour off the fat.) Add the shallots and cook for 3 minutes. Add the vinegar, bring to a boil, and cook for 3 minutes. Off the heat, add the remaining ¼ cup of olive oil, 2 teaspoons salt, and 1 teaspoon pepper.

Meanwhile, remove the core of the frisée (see note), wash, and spin-dry. Chop the frisée into large bite-size pieces and transfer to a large bowl. Pour the warm dressing and bacon over the frisée and add the croutons. Toss well, taste for seasonings, and divide among four large plates. Top each with a jammy egg cut in half. Sprinkle with salt and serve warm.

To prep the frisée, flatten the leaves and cut around the core.

jammy eggs

MAKES 4 EGGS

4 extra-large eggs

Fill a medium saucepan with water and bring to a boil. With a spoon, carefully lower each egg into the boiling water. Lower the heat until the water is at a gentle simmer; you don't want the eggs knocking around in the boiling water or they will crack. Cook the eggs for 6½ minutes exactly, then remove them from the saucepan, run them under cool water, and peel. You can hold the peeled eggs at room temperature for up to an hour.

PREP AHEAD

baked croque monsieurs

SERVES 4

We all love a croque monsieur, which is basically a French ham and cheese sandwich. This fancy variation is made with croissants (always a good idea!) baked in a savory custard. You assemble the whole dish a day in advance and bake it just before lunch.

- 4 plain all-butter croissants, preferably one or two days old
- 4 tablespoons good Dijon mustard, such as Grey Poupon
- 4 medium-thick slices Black Forest ham
- 2½ cups grated Gruyère cheese (about 8 ounces), divided (see note)
- 1¼ cups whole milk
- ½ cup heavy cream
- 4 extra-large eggs
- Kosher salt and freshly ground black pepper

One day ahead, slice each croissant in half horizontally with a serrated knife. Spread the cut side of each bottom half evenly with 1 tablespoon of mustard. Place one slice of ham on top, folding it to fit, and sprinkle each with ½ cup of the Gruyère. Cover with the top halves of the croissants, cut sides down, and place the croissants very snugly in a 9 × 12 or 10 × 13-inch oval baking dish, depending on the size of the croissants.

Measure the milk and cream in a 4-cup measuring cup. Whisk in the eggs, 2 teaspoons salt, and 1 teaspoon pepper and pour over the croissants. Cover with plastic wrap and refrigerate overnight.

The next day, preheat the oven to 350 degrees. Sprinkle the remaining ½ cup Gruyère on the croissants and bake for 30 to 35 minutes, until a knife inserted in the middle of the custard comes out clean. If the croissants are getting too brown, cover loosely with aluminum foil. Serve hot.

You can grate the cheese either by hand on the carrot grating side of a box grater or by using a food processor fitted with the grating disk.

REALLY FAST

cheddar & chive omelet

MAKES ONE OMELET

I have spent countless hours (and eggs!) trying to make a perfect omelet, but a video of Jacques Pépin making an omelet taught me three important details. First, add water to the eggs to make them light and tender. Second, use butter and oil in the pan so the omelet doesn't brown. And finally, instead of flipping the omelet, fold it like an envelope and then turn it out upside down onto the plate. Voilà—the perfect omelet!

3 extra-large eggs
Kosher salt and freshly ground black pepper
1 tablespoon minced fresh chives, plus extra for serving
1 tablespoon unsalted butter
1 tablespoon canola oil
½ cup grated aged Cheddar

Prep all of the ingredients before you start cooking. Place the eggs, 1 tablespoon water, ½ teaspoon salt, and ¼ teaspoon pepper in a bowl and beat them vigorously with a fork. Stir in the tablespoon of chives.

Put the butter and oil in a 9-inch nonstick omelet or crêpe pan over medium heat. Just before the butter completely melts, pour in the egg mixture. While shaking the pan back and forth on the stove, rapidly stir the eggs with the fork (as though you were making scrambled eggs) for 60 to 75 seconds, until the eggs are almost—but not totally—cooked.

Spread the mixture out evenly with the fork and allow the omelet to sit on the heat for 10 seconds ***only*** for a thin skin of eggs to form on the bottom of the omelet. Meanwhile, sprinkle the Cheddar down the middle of the omelet. With a rubber spatula, fold the sides of the omelet over the filling like folding a letter—first one side over the cheese and then the other side over. Invert the omelet onto a plate, sprinkle with chives, salt, and pepper, and serve hot.

If you're making a few omelets, have all the egg mixtures and other ingredients prepped before you start cooking the first one.

endive & avocado salad

SERVES 6

One of my favorite restaurants in NYC is Cipriani. It's both elegant and simple at the same time. This salad is delicious, and the only "cooking" is stirring together the dressing. With so few ingredients, it's important to use freshly squeezed lemon juice; lemon loses its citrusy edge in less than a day.

½ cup freshly squeezed lemon juice (2 to 3 lemons)
½ cup good olive oil
Kosher salt and freshly ground black pepper
4 medium heads Belgian endive
3 ripe Hass avocados, peeled and pitted (see note)
1 cup shaved Italian Parmesan cheese

Hass avocados are the ones with dark brown skins when ripe. The smooth green ones don't have as much flavor.

In a small glass measuring cup, measure the lemon juice and olive oil. Add 2 teaspoons salt and 1 teaspoon pepper and whisk together. Set aside.

Remove a ½ inch from the stem end of each endive. Cut the endive crosswise in 1-inch chunks, separating the leaves and discarding the core as you go, and place in a serving bowl. Cut the avocados in ¾-inch dice (you could also slice them thickly) and add to the bowl. Add enough vinaigrette to moisten and toss lightly. Sprinkle the Parmesan on top, then carefully fold the Parmesan into the salad. Taste for seasonings and serve at room temperature.

MAKE AHEAD

roasted cauliflower salad

SERVES 6

Round Swamp Farm is a wonderful specialty food store in East Hampton. This salad was inspired by their roasted cauliflower salad. Roasting the cauliflower with butter and seasonings makes it so much more flavorful than boiling it in water. Make the salad early and let it sit at room temperature.

2 pounds cauliflower (1 large or 2 small heads)
2 tablespoons unsalted butter, melted
Kosher salt and freshly ground black pepper
¼ cup good white wine vinegar
1 tablespoon good Dijon mustard, such as Grey Poupon
Good olive oil
1 tablespoon store-bought pesto
½ cup plump dried tart cherries
4 cups baby arugula (4 to 5 ounces)
½ cup toasted pine nuts (see note)
1 cup shaved Italian Parmesan cheese (4 ounces)
Juice of 1 lemon

Preheat the oven to 425 degrees. Cut the cauliflower into florets and discard the stems. Cut each floret in half or thirds, depending on the size. Place them on a sheet pan and toss with the melted butter, 1 teaspoon salt, and ½ teaspoon pepper. Roast for 15 to 17 minutes, tossing once, until tender and nicely browned.

Meanwhile, in a small glass measuring cup, whisk together the vinegar, mustard, ½ teaspoon salt, and ¼ teaspoon pepper. While whisking, slowly pour in ⅓ cup olive oil. Set aside.

Transfer the hot cauliflower to a large serving bowl and pour on the vinaigrette. Add the pesto and cherries and toss well. Set aside to cool.

When ready to serve, add the arugula and sprinkle with salt. Add the pine nuts, Parmesan, and lemon juice. Toss well and serve at room temperature.

To toast pine nuts, place them in a dry sauté pan and cook over low heat for 10 minutes, tossing often, until lightly browned.

ASSEMBLED

real greek salad

This is how a Greek salad would be served in Greece. I like to serve it with a vinaigrette because the oregano and garlic enhance the flavor, but you can also do as they do in Greece; just sprinkle the salad with salt and black pepper and put bottles of olive oil and vinegar on the table so people can help themselves. Make a big platter with really good ingredients and everyone will love it!

Red heirloom tomatoes, cored and cut into wedges
Green bell pepper, sliced crosswise in rounds, seeded
Hothouse cucumbers, unpeeled, sliced ¼-inch thick
Small red onion, thinly sliced
Kalamata olives, pitted
Pepperoncini in vinegar, such as Krinos, drained
Capers in brine, drained
Thickly sliced feta, preferably Greek
Fresh oregano (optional)

FOR THE VINAIGRETTE

¼ cup good red wine vinegar
½ cup good olive oil
½ teaspoon dried oregano, crushed in your hands
2 garlic cloves, grated on a rasp
Kosher salt and freshly ground black pepper

Arrange the tomatoes, bell peppers, cucumbers, onions, olives, pepperoncini, and capers on a large platter. Lay slices of feta on top and sprinkle with small fresh oregano leaves (if using).

In a small glass measuring cup, whisk together the vinegar, olive oil, dried oregano, garlic, 1 teaspoon salt, and ½ teaspoon black pepper. Drizzle over the salad just before serving.

dinner

provençal chicken
with olives & capers

sesame ginger chicken bowl

chicken souvlaki & tzatziki

mustard-roasted meatballs

roast duck legs
with cherry sauce

apricot-glazed corned beef

strip steak
with roquefort chive butter

french sausage & lentils

balsamic grilled flank steak

contents *continue* >>>

easy lobster bake

roasted cod
with brown butter & capers

roasted halibut
with potato chip crust

crabmeat gratins

skillet pasta
with sausage & mozzarella

orecchiette *with sweet corn*

lemon capellini primavera

one-pot dinners

I know they're incredibly popular, but I just don't love sheet pan dinners. They're easy but are they *really* delicious? What I find interesting in a dish is the layers of flavor in each bite—how each ingredient makes every other one taste better. I find I can achieve more of those satisfying flavors by cooking everything together in one pot, and it's frankly just as easy as throwing them on a sheet pan.

Here's an example. One night, I made a sheet pan roast chicken with herbes de Provence plus shallots and olives for dinner. Sounds good, right? But it was beyond boring. And I realized why—nothing on that sheet pan flavored anything else. It was just chicken, shallots, and olives. It was like conducting an orchestra but instead of all the instruments playing a symphony together, the violin, the flute, and the clarinet were all playing solos at the same time. The chicken tasted like

chicken, the shallots like shallots, and the olives like olives, but the shallots didn't flavor the chicken, and the olives didn't flavor anything.

The next day, I put all of the same ingredients for the Provençal Chicken with Olives & Capers (page 97) into a big Le Creuset pot instead of spreading them out on a sheet pan. I seared the chicken to caramelize the skin before adding the herbes de Provence, shallots, garlic, some white wine, olives, and capers for a little acidity. The chicken and sauce were all imbued with those Provençal flavors after simmering away in the oven for about 50 minutes. If you serve it with some brown rice or Garlic Mashed Potatoes (page 151), you've got a dinner with extraordinary depth of flavor that you'd be proud to serve your mother-in-law. One pot instead of one sheet pan and it has so much more flavor.

using heirloom dishes and linens in a modern way

We all have beautiful antique dishes that we've either inherited or bought at flea markets or tag sales. They're often an odd number of dishes in unmatched patterns, and it's difficult to figure out how to use them. In fact, I love combining unmatched dishes for a casual but elegant table. The trick is to have simple modern (and matching) plates underneath and then choose two or three patterns of china plates to use on top. The effect can be curated and elegant but also casual.

MAKE AHEAD

provençal chicken
with olives & capers

SERVES 4 TO 6

This chicken has all the classic flavors of Provence: shallots, garlic, olives, and herbes de Provence. Make it early in the day and reheat it for dinner. No sweat!

- 8 bone-in, skin-on chicken thighs
- Kosher salt and freshly ground black pepper
- All-purpose flour
- Good olive oil
- 6 medium shallots, peeled and halved through the root end
- 10 to 12 garlic cloves
- 1 cup dry white wine, such as Chablis
- 1 tablespoon herbes de Provence (preferably without lavender; see note)
- 1 cup large pitted green olives in brine, such as Cerignola, drained
- 2 tablespoons capers in brine, drained

MAKE AHEAD: *Prepare the dish completely, refrigerate, and reheat over medium-low heat on top of the stove.*

Herbes de Provence is a blend of flavors, and I find those that contain lavender taste more like soap than food.

Preheat the oven to 325 degrees.

Place the chicken thighs on a plate and sprinkle all over with 2½ teaspoons salt and 1½ teaspoons pepper. Dredge them in flour, shaking off the excess.

Heat ¼ cup olive oil in a medium (10 to 11-inch) Dutch oven, such as Le Creuset, over medium-high heat. Place half of the chicken pieces in the pot, skin side down, and cook for 4 to 5 minutes, turning once, until the chicken is nicely browned. Remove to a plate and repeat with the remaining chicken.

Lower the heat to medium, put the shallots and garlic in the pot, and cook for 5 minutes, stirring occasionally. Return the chicken to the pot, skin side up, and add the wine. Add the herbes de Provence, olives, and capers and cover the pot.

Bake for 45 to 50 minutes, until the chicken is 160 degrees when tested with a thermometer. Sprinkle with salt and serve hot with the vegetables and sauce.

PREP AHEAD

sesame ginger chicken bowl

SERVES 3

I love one-bowl dinners, especially those I can prep ahead. This chicken marinates in the refrigerator for up to 6 hours and just needs a quick stir-fry before serving. And since I use my rice cooker, which makes cooking rice foolproof, this has become an easy weeknight dinner.

- 3 tablespoons soy sauce, such as Kikkoman (not low-sodium)
- 2 tablespoons pure maple syrup
- 5 tablespoons rice vinegar, divided
- 2 tablespoons toasted sesame oil
- 4 large garlic cloves, grated (see note)
- 1½ teaspoons peeled and finely grated fresh ginger (see note)
- ½ teaspoon crushed red pepper flakes
- Kosher salt and freshly ground black pepper
- 1½ pounds boneless, skinless chicken thighs, 2-inch diced
- 1 hothouse cucumber, unpeeled and thinly sliced crosswise (see note)
- ½ cup thinly sliced shallots (2 large)
- 2 tablespoons canola oil
- Sesame seeds, toasted (see note, page 147)
- Cooked white basmati rice, for serving

I use a rasp to grate the garlic and ginger and an OXO mandoline to slice the cucumber.

In a large bowl, combine the soy sauce, maple syrup, 3 tablespoons of the vinegar, the sesame oil, garlic, ginger, red pepper flakes, and 1 teaspoon salt. Add the chicken, stir well, cover, and refrigerate for at least 1 hour or up to 6 hours.

In a medium bowl, combine the cucumber, shallots, the remaining 2 tablespoons of vinegar, ½ teaspoon salt, and ¼ teaspoon black pepper. Set aside for 10 minutes or refrigerate for up to a day.

When ready to serve, heat the canola oil in a large (12-inch) sauté pan over medium-high heat. When the oil is hot, lift the chicken out of the marinade with a slotted spoon (reserve the marinade) and transfer to the pan. Cook for 2 minutes without moving, turn each piece, and cook for 2 minutes on the other side. Add the reserved marinade, lower the heat, and cook, stirring occasionally, for 2 minutes, until the chicken is just cooked through and the sauce is reduced. Serve the hot rice in shallow bowls with the hot chicken, sauce, and cucumbers on top. Sprinkle with the sesame seeds and salt.

SHORTCUT

chicken souvlaki & tzatziki

SERVES 4

This dinner comes together so easily—while the skewers soak in water, you marinate the chicken, and while that marinates, you fire up the grill. The chicken gets so much flavor from the grill, and the store-bought tzatziki makes it easy.

4 to 6 (9 to 11-inch) bamboo skewers
Finely grated zest of 1 large lemon, grated on a rasp
¼ cup freshly squeezed lemon juice (2 lemons)
2 large garlic cloves, grated on a rasp
1½ teaspoons dried oregano
Kosher salt and freshly ground black pepper
Good olive oil
1½ pounds boneless, skinless chicken breasts, 1-inch diced
1 small zucchini, trimmed and cut into ½-inch-thick rounds
1 large red or yellow Holland bell pepper, stemmed, seeded, and 1-inch diced
1 small red onion, half 1-inch diced and half cut in slivers for serving
Pita bread and lemon wedges, for serving
Store-bought tzatziki, such as Cedar's, for serving

Soak the skewers in water for 45 minutes. Meanwhile, in a large bowl, whisk together the lemon zest, lemon juice, garlic, oregano, 2 teaspoons salt, and 1 teaspoon pepper. Whisk in ⅓ cup olive oil. Add the chicken, zucchini, bell pepper, and diced red onions, and toss well. Set aside for ***only*** 20 minutes (the lemon juice will break down the chicken if you marinate it longer).

Meanwhile, prepare a gas or charcoal grill to cook over medium heat. (You can also use the broiler or a grill pan.)

Thread the marinated vegetables and chicken snugly on the skewers—first two vegetables, then three chicken, then two vegetables, then three chicken. Repeat until the skewers are filled. Place the skewers on a plate and pour any remaining marinade over them.

Grill the skewers over medium heat for 8 to 10 minutes, turning every 2 minutes, until the chicken and vegetables are nicely charred and the chicken is *almost done*. (Don't overcook the chicken or it will be dry.) Sprinkle with salt, cover loosely with foil, and allow to rest for 5 minutes. Meanwhile, grill or toast the pitas for one minute on each side, until warmed.

Place one pita on each plate, spread very generously with the tzatziki, place one or two skewers on top, and add a few slivers of red onion. Serve warm with a lemon wedge.

MAKE AHEAD

mustard-roasted meatballs

MAKES 18 TO 20 LARGE MEATBALLS

Really good meatballs are so versatile; I like to make a big tray at a time so I can keep some in the freezer. It's so much easier to roast the meatballs than to fry them, not to mention you don't have to clean the stove and kitchen afterwards. I like to serve them with creamy polenta, but they're also good with spaghetti and tomato sauce or in a meatball hero.

2 extra-large eggs
1 cup whole milk
¼ cup whole grain mustard
3 cups fresh white breadcrumbs (see note)
½ cup freshly grated Italian Parmesan cheese
½ cup freshly grated Italian Pecorino cheese
2 tablespoons dried Italian seasoning
¼ cup minced fresh parsley
½ teaspoon crushed red pepper flakes
Kosher salt and freshly ground black pepper
1 pound lean ground pork
½ pound sweet Italian sausage, casings removed
½ pound hot Italian sausage, casings removed

For fresh breadcrumbs, remove the crusts of Pepperidge Farm white bread, dice the bread, and process in a food processor fitted with the steel blade.

Preheat the oven to 425 degrees. Line a sheet pan with parchment paper.

In a large bowl, whisk the eggs, milk, and mustard until well blended. Add the breadcrumbs and let them soak in the liquid for 10 minutes. Add the Parmesan, Pecorino, Italian seasoning, parsley, red pepper flakes, 2 teaspoons salt, and 1 teaspoon black pepper and combine.

Meanwhile, with clean hands, combine the pork and sausage in a large bowl (don't overmix!). Add the breadcrumb mixture to the meat mixture and combine well without compacting it.

With a standard 2¼-inch ice cream scoop, form rounded scoops of the mixture and place them on the prepared sheet pan. Roast for 30 to 35 minutes, until browned and cooked through. Serve immediately or cool, wrap well, and refrigerate for up to 4 days or freeze for up to 3 months.

SHORTCUT

roast duck legs with cherry sauce

SERVES 6

Duck confit is a classic French dish of duck legs cooked for hours with aromatics and salt in their own rendered fat until they are falling-off-the-bone tender. It's really time-consuming to make, so it was a revelation that I could just order duck confit from D'Artagnan and crisp it in the oven. The red currant and mustard sauce with cherries couldn't be easier.

6 duck legs confit, such as D'Artagnan
1½ cups red currant jelly (18 ounces), such as Tiptree
¼ cup good Dijon mustard, such as Grey Poupon
Kosher salt and freshly ground black pepper
½ cup dried cherries

Preheat the oven to 450 degrees.

Heat a large (12-inch) dry cast-iron skillet over medium heat for 2 minutes. Place the duck legs in the pan, skin side down, and sear for 2 minutes. Turn the legs and roast in the oven for 15 minutes. Turn the legs skin side down again and roast for another 5 minutes.

Meanwhile, combine the red currant jelly, Dijon mustard, ½ teaspoon salt, and ¼ teaspoon pepper in a small saucepan and warm over medium heat until the jelly melts completely. Add the cherries and cook for 2 more minutes.

Serve the duck legs crispy skin side up with the sauce spooned over the top.

PREP AHEAD

apricot-glazed corned beef

SERVES 4 TO 6

When I first met Jeffrey, he came to my house for dinner and my mother made corned beef. Of course, he said it was delicious (it wasn't). After that, every time Jeffrey came for dinner, my mother made what she thought was his "favorite" corned beef. Poor guy! If she had made this one with apricot jam and lots of mustard, he actually would have loved it! You can cook the corned beef up to a day ahead and roast it before serving.

- 1 corned beef brisket (about 4 pounds; discard the seasoning packet)
- 1 cup apricot jam
- 2 tablespoons runny honey
- 1½ tablespoons good Dijon mustard, such as Grey Poupon
- 1½ tablespoons whole grain mustard
- 1½ tablespoons honey mustard, such as Honeycup

Place the corned beef in a very large pot of boiling salted water, cover, and reduce the heat. Simmer for 3½ to 4 hours, until very tender when tested with a fork.

Preheat the oven to 350 degrees. Line a sheet pan with aluminum foil.

In a medium bowl, whisk together the apricot jam, honey, Dijon mustard, whole grain mustard, and honey mustard. Drain the corned beef and place it fat side up on the prepared sheet pan. Spoon ⅔ of the mustard glaze on the top and sides of the corned beef. Bake for 30 minutes, until the glaze is bubbling and beginning to brown. Allow to rest for 5 minutes, slice it across the grain (see note), and serve hot with the remaining glaze on the side.

It's sometimes hard to figure out what "across the grain" means. If the meat separates into long shreds when you slice it, you are slicing with the grain; turn it 90 degrees and slice it in the other direction to slice across the grain.

PREP AHEAD

strip steak with roquefort chive butter

SERVES 6

I learned how to make foolproof grilled steaks from the famous NYC butcher Lobel's. If you follow the directions exactly, these will come out perfectly every time. The Roquefort butter makes them really special.

3 (18 to 20-ounce) New York strip steaks, 1½ inches thick
Good olive oil
Kosher salt and coarsely ground black pepper
Roquefort Chive Butter, at room temperature
Chopped fresh chives, for serving

Pat the steaks dry with paper towels. Brush them all over with olive oil. Combine 2 tablespoons salt and 1 tablespoon pepper and pat the mixture all over the steaks. Allow to sit at room temperature for one hour.

Prepare a charcoal grill with medium-hot coals on one side of the grill and no coals on the other side. Sear the steaks on the hot side of the grill for exactly 2 minutes on each side. Transfer the steaks to the cool side of the grill and close the lid, making sure the vents are open so the fire doesn't go out. Cook the steaks for 7 to 8 minutes, until the internal temperature is 115 to 120 degrees for rare and 125 degrees for medium. Transfer the steaks to a platter, cover them loosely with aluminum foil, and allow to rest for 10 minutes.

Slice the steaks thickly and top with thick slices of the Roquefort Chive Butter. Sprinkle with chives and some salt and serve warm.

roquefort chive butter

MAKES 2 CUPS

½ pound (2 sticks) unsalted butter, at room temperature
6 ounces Roquefort cheese, at room temperature
Kosher salt and freshly ground black pepper
¼ cup minced fresh chives

Place the butter, Roquefort, 1½ teaspoons salt, and 1 teaspoon pepper in the bowl of an electric mixer fitted with the paddle attachment. Beat on low speed until combined. Stir in the chives.

With a rubber spatula, transfer the butter mixture to a sheet of parchment paper. Shape the mixture loosely into a log approximately 1 inch in diameter by 12 inches long. Roll the paper around the butter, pressing to shape it into a compact, round cylinder. Refrigerate for up to a week or freeze for up to 3 months. Serve at room temperature.

MAKE AHEAD

french sausage & lentils

SERVES 3 TO 4

When you are cooking simply, extraordinary ingredients really matter. French sausage is more finely ground than Italian sausage and has a more refined flavor. This is an earthy and satisfying dinner on a cold winter night.

Good olive oil

2 cups chopped leeks, white and light green parts (1 large), washed and spun dry

1½ cups scrubbed and (½-inch) diced carrots (2 to 3 carrots)

1 tablespoon minced garlic (3 cloves)

1 cup French green Le Puy lentils

4 cups boiling water

1 yellow onion, peeled and stuck with 6 whole dried cloves

1 white turnip, cut in half

1 teaspoon unsalted butter

4 teaspoons good Dijon mustard, such as Grey Poupon, plus extra for serving

2 tablespoons good red wine vinegar

Kosher salt and freshly ground black pepper

1 pound D'Artagnan French garlic sausage, sliced ½-inch thick

Heat 2 tablespoons olive oil in a small (9-inch) pot or Dutch oven, such as Le Creuset. Add the leeks and carrots and cook over medium heat for 5 minutes, stirring occasionally, until softened. Add the garlic and cook for one minute. Add the lentils, boiling water, onion with cloves, and turnip and simmer for 20 minutes, until the lentils are tender. Discard the onion and turnip. Drain the lentils and transfer to a medium bowl. Stir in the butter.

Meanwhile, whisk together ¼ cup olive oil, the mustard, vinegar, 4 teaspoons salt, and 1 teaspoon pepper. Stir into the hot lentils.

Meanwhile, heat 2 tablespoons olive oil in a large (12-inch) sauté pan over medium heat. Add the sausage to the pan and sear on each side for 2 minutes, until browned and heated through. Spoon the lentils onto dinner plates or a serving platter, arrange the sausage on top, and serve hot with extra mustard.

MAKE AHEAD: *You can prepare the lentils early in the day and refrigerate them. Sear the sausage and reheat the lentils just before serving.*

PREP AHEAD

balsamic grilled flank steak

SERVES 4 TO 6

Flank steak is a terrific cut of meat—it's not as expensive as a rib eye and has great flavor. I marinate it, grill it, and slice it thinly on the diagonal across the grain. A drizzle of syrupy vinegar before serving makes it even better.

Good olive oil

2 tablespoons coarsely chopped fresh rosemary leaves, plus extra for serving

2 tablespoons syrupy aged balsamic vinegar, such as Villa Manodori, plus extra for serving

1½ tablespoons coarsely chopped garlic (5 cloves)

1 tablespoon good Dijon mustard, such as Grey Poupon

Kosher salt and freshly ground black pepper

1 (1¾ to 2-pound) flank steak

Flake sea salt, such as Maldon

Place ⅓ cup olive oil, the rosemary, vinegar, garlic, mustard, 2 teaspoons kosher salt, and 1 teaspoon pepper in a food processor or blender and purée for 30 to 45 seconds, until thick and smooth.

Score the top of the steak with a sharp knife in a 1-inch crisscross pattern, cutting only about ⅛ inch deep. Place the steak flat in a nonreactive dish. Spread the marinade on the steak, turning to coat both sides. Cover and refrigerate for at least 2 hours or up to 24 hours.

Prepare a gas or charcoal grill to cook over medium-high heat. (I spread hot coals two layers deep.) Brush the grill grate with oil. When the grill is hot, cook the steak over direct heat for exactly 4 minutes on each side for medium-rare. Transfer to a carving board, cover with foil, and allow to rest for 5 to 10 minutes.

Carve the steak in thin slices diagonally across the grain. Sprinkle with extra rosemary and sea salt and drizzle with more balsamic vinegar. Serve warm.

easy lobster bake

SERVES 6

This is an old-fashioned Maine casserole dish updated with sherry, panko, and fresh tarragon. Prepare the gratin dishes early in the day, refrigerate them, and bake them just before serving. Hard to imagine something so elegant and delicious could be so easy, and yet it is!

- 10 tablespoons (5 ounces) good salted butter, such as Kerrygold, divided
- ¼ cup freshly squeezed lemon juice (2 lemons)
- ¼ cup cream sherry, such as Harvey's Bristol Cream
- 2 pounds uncooked lobster meat, cut into large, bite-size chunks (see note)
- 12 original Ritz crackers
- ⅔ cup panko (Japanese bread flakes)
- 2 teaspoons minced garlic (2 cloves)
- 3 tablespoons coarsely chopped fresh flat-leaf parsley
- 2 teaspoons coarsely chopped fresh tarragon leaves
- Kosher salt and freshly ground black pepper
- Flake sea salt, such as Maldon, and lemon wedges, for serving

Preheat the oven to 375 degrees. Arrange two racks evenly spaced in the oven. Place 6 gratin dishes on two sheet pans.

Melt 6 tablespoons of the butter in a medium (10-inch) sauté pan over medium-low heat. Swirl in the lemon juice and sherry. Add the lobster, tossing gently to coat with the butter mixture. Allow the lobster to cook for just 3 minutes. Turn off the heat.

Meanwhile, melt the remaining 4 tablespoons of butter. Crumble the Ritz crackers into the bowl of a food processor fitted with the steel blade. Add the panko, garlic, parsley, and tarragon and process until the ingredients are crumbs. Add the melted butter, 2 teaspoons kosher salt, and 1 teaspoon pepper and pulse to just moisten the crumbs.

Spoon the lobster and the juices evenly into the gratin dishes and sprinkle the crumb mixture evenly on top, allowing some crumbs to fall into the sauce. Bake for 13 to 15 minutes, until the juices are bubbling and the crumbs are lightly browned. Sprinkle with sea salt and serve hot with a lemon wedge.

If your seafood shop doesn't sell uncooked lobster meat, you can buy uncooked lobster tails. You'll need 4 pounds of lobster tails in the shell to yield 2 pounds of lobster meat. Cut the shell with kitchen shears and break it open with your hands to remove the meat.

roasted cod with brown butter & capers

SERVES 3

This recipe is inspired by both Eric Ripert of Le Bernardin and Erin French of The Lost Kitchen. If you're going to cook more than 3 fillets, you'll need a second pan.

Good olive oil
3 (8-ounce) boneless center-cut cod fillets, skin removed
Kosher salt and freshly ground black pepper
Wondra flour
4 tablespoons salted European butter, such as Plugrà, large-diced
¼ cup capers in brine, drained
Minced fresh parsley and freshly squeezed lemon juice, for serving

Preheat the oven to 425 degrees.

Heat a large (12-inch) dry cast-iron skillet over medium-high heat for 2 minutes. Add 3 tablespoons olive oil and heat until it starts to smoke.

Meanwhile, dry the fillets with paper towels then sprinkle them on both sides with 1 teaspoon salt and ½ teaspoon pepper. Dust the fish all over with Wondra flour, shaking off the excess. Place the fillets in the pan (don't crowd them!) and cook for 3 minutes without moving them, until nicely browned on one side. Turn the fish gently with a metal spatula and add the butter and capers to the pan. Place the skillet in the oven and cook for 4 to 5 minutes, depending on the thickness of the fish, just until the fish is firm when touched in the middle.

Spoon the brown butter and capers on the fish, cover with foil, and allow to rest for 5 minutes. (It will finish cooking while it rests.) Sprinkle with the parsley and lemon juice and serve hot.

REALLY FAST

roasted halibut with potato chip crust

SERVES 4

Halibut and potato chips reminds me of both fancy halibut wrapped in a crispy potato crust and simple fish and chips, but this version doesn't require a mandoline or a deep fryer.

- ⅔ cup good mayonnaise, such as Hellmann's
- ⅓ cup minced shallot (1 large)
- 1 tablespoon minced fresh dill
- 1½ teaspoons good Dijon mustard, such as Grey Poupon
- Kosher salt and freshly ground black pepper
- ½ cup coarsely crushed ridged potato chips, such as Cape Cod
- ½ cup panko (Japanese bread flakes)
- Good olive oil
- 4 (6-ounce) skin-on center-cut halibut fillets
- 2 tablespoons freshly squeezed lemon juice, plus lemon wedges for serving

Preheat the oven to 425 degrees. Place a piece of parchment paper on a sheet pan. (If your fillets don't have skin, don't use parchment or the fish will stick. Just place the fish directly on the sheet pan.)

In a small bowl, stir together the mayonnaise, shallots, dill, mustard, 1 teaspoon salt, and ½ teaspoon pepper. In a separate bowl, combine the potato chips, panko, and 1 tablespoon olive oil.

Dry the halibut fillets with paper towels and arrange them on the prepared sheet pan, skin side down. Drizzle the lemon juice on the fillets and sprinkle with 1 teaspoon salt and ½ teaspoon pepper. Spread the mayonnaise mixture very thickly on the fillets. (It will seem like a lot but use it all.) Spoon the panko mixture evenly on top.

Bake for 13 to 15 minutes, until the topping is browned and the fish is just cooked in the center. Remove the fish from the parchment paper with a large spatula, leaving the skin on the paper. Serve hot with the lemon wedges.

SHORTCUT

crabmeat gratins

SERVES 6

The magic of crabmeat is that it comes already cooked and ready to eat. You can prep these gratins early in the day, add the topping, and bake them right before dinner. I combine one pound each of jumbo and regular lump crabmeat to have both textures.

- 2 cups good mayonnaise, such as Hellmann's
- 6 extra-large egg yolks
- 5½ teaspoons Old Bay seasoning, divided
- 1½ teaspoons grated lemon zest, plus extra for serving
- 4 teaspoons freshly squeezed lemon juice
- 2 cups freshly grated Gruyère cheese, divided (6 ounces with rind)
- Kosher salt and freshly ground black pepper
- 2 pounds very good fresh lump crabmeat, undrained (see headnote)
- 1 cup thinly sliced scallions, green and white parts (5 to 7 scallions)
- 1⅓ cups panko (Japanese bread flakes)
- 3 tablespoons coarsely chopped fresh flat-leaf parsley
- 4 tablespoons (½ stick) unsalted butter, melted

Preheat the oven to 350 degrees. Arrange two racks evenly spaced in the oven. Place six (6-inch) gratin dishes on two sheet pans.

In a large bowl, combine the mayonnaise, egg yolks, 4 teaspoons of the Old Bay seasoning, the lemon zest, lemon juice, 1 cup of the Gruyère, 1 tablespoon salt, and 1½ teaspoons pepper. Gently stir in the crabmeat and scallions and transfer to the gratin dishes.

Place the panko, parsley, the remaining 1½ teaspoons of Old Bay seasoning, remaining 1 cup of Gruyère, and the melted butter in a food processor and pulse just 6 times to moisten the mixture. Sprinkle evenly on the gratins. Bake for 35 to 40 minutes, until the tops are golden brown, switching the sheet pans halfway through. Grate some lemon zest on top and serve hot.

SHORTCUT

skillet pasta with sausage & mozzarella

SERVES 4 TO 5

This is the ultimate comfort dinner. I make it in a large sauté pan and then just bring the whole pan to the table for people to help themselves. A good jarred marinara sauce like Rao's makes this so easy. If you like, add a large dollop of fresh ricotta to each serving.

- Kosher salt and freshly ground black pepper
- Good olive oil
- ½ pound ground sirloin
- ½ pound sweet or spicy Italian sausage, casings removed
- 1 (24-ounce) jar Rao's marinara sauce
- ⅓ cup heavy cream
- ¼ cup good Italian red wine, such as Chianti
- ½ teaspoon crushed red pepper flakes
- ¾ pound penne, such as De Cecco
- 1 cup small fresh mozzarella balls (bocconcini), halved
- ½ cup freshly grated Italian Parmesan cheese, plus extra for serving
- ⅓ cup julienned fresh basil leaves, plus extra for serving

Bring a large pot of water with 2 tablespoons of salt to a boil.

Meanwhile, heat 1½ tablespoons olive oil over medium heat in a large (12-inch) sauté pan. Add the ground beef and sausage and cook for 5 to 7 minutes, breaking them up with a fork, until they begin to brown. Stir in the marinara sauce and simmer for 10 minutes. Stir the cream, wine, red pepper flakes, 1 teaspoon salt, and 1 teaspoon black pepper into the pasta sauce and simmer for 2 minutes.

Add the pasta to the boiling water and cook for 10 minutes, until almost al dente. (It will cook more in the sauce.)

With a wire strainer, lift the pasta out of the water (bringing some water with it) and add it to the pasta sauce. Add ⅓ cup of the pasta cooking water and simmer for 3 minutes. Off the heat, add the mozzarella, Parmesan, and basil. Serve hot in bowls sprinkled with salt, Parmesan, and some basil.

MAKE AHEAD: *Prepare the sauce ahead but don't cook the pasta until you're ready to serve the dinner. Reheat the sauce in a skillet, add the cooked pasta, and finish the recipe.*

SHORTCUT

orecchiette with sweet corn

SERVES 6

I was testing the recipe for Sautéed Corn with Pesto & Parmesan when my assistants Rose and Mica both mentioned they make pasta with fresh corn for dinner. I added orecchiette (little ears) to the pot to catch the kernels of corn, and a side was transformed into a main dish. Store-bought pesto streamlines the whole process.

1 recipe Sautéed Corn with Pesto & Parmesan (page 139)
Kosher salt and freshly ground black pepper
1 pound orecchiette pasta, such as De Cecco
1 tablespoon store-bought pesto
¼ cup julienned fresh basil leaves, plus extra for serving

Prepare the Sautéed Corn with Pesto & Parmesan, omitting the fresh basil. Set aside in the pan until the pasta is cooked.

Meanwhile, boil a large pot of water, add 2 tablespoons of salt, and add the orecchiette. Cook for 9 to 11 minutes (or according to the instructions on the package), until barely al dente. Do not drain.

Lift the pasta out of the water with a large strainer or spider and add it directly to the pan with the corn, bringing some of the pasta water with it. Heat the corn and pasta together over medium-low heat, adding ½ cup of the cooking water, the pesto, 2 teaspoons salt, and 1 teaspoon pepper. Stir in the julienned basil leaves, taste for seasonings, and serve hot with more basil sprinkled on top.

REALLY EASY

lemon capellini primavera

SERVES 6

The Lemon Capellini with Caviar in my first book, The Barefoot Contessa Cookbook, *is so delicious and easy that I wanted to do an everyday version. This one has lots of green vegetables instead of caviar. The lemon zest, chives, and dill give it so much flavor.*

2 cups asparagus (bottoms trimmed), cut diagonally in 2-inch lengths

2 cups sugar snap peas (strings removed), cut in thirds diagonally

⅓ cup minced fresh chives, plus extra for garnish

⅓ cup minced fresh dill, plus extra for garnish

½ pound (2 sticks) unsalted butter

Zest and juice of 2 large lemons, plus extra zest for serving

Kosher salt and freshly ground black pepper

1 teaspoon minced garlic

1 pound dried capellini

1 cup frozen green peas

Place the asparagus and snap peas in a bowl. Place the chives and dill in a second bowl and set them both aside.

Put the butter, lemon zest, lemon juice, 2 teaspoons salt, and 1 teaspoon pepper in a large (12-inch) sauté pan over medium heat and heat just until the butter melts. Add the garlic, cook for 30 seconds, and remove from the heat.

Meanwhile, bring a large pot of water with 2 tablespoons of salt to a rolling boil. Add the capellini and cook for 2 to 4 minutes, until al dente. With tongs, transfer the pasta to the sauté pan and simmer over medium-low heat for one minute, stirring and adding some of the pasta water as needed to make a light sauce. Put the mixed asparagus and snap peas into the pasta water and cook for one minute. Add the frozen peas to the pot, then immediately transfer all the vegetables to the pasta with a sieve or slotted spoon; don't drain the water. Add the chives and dill to the pasta and toss well.

Continue to simmer the pasta for one minute, adding more pasta water as necessary to maintain the sauce. Garnish with extra chives, dill, salt, and pepper. Grate some lemon zest on top and serve hot.

sides

roasted asparagus
with parmesan panko

chipotle maple mashed sweet potatoes

sautéed corn
with pesto & parmesan

caramelized butternut squash
& cranberries

maple & balsamic roasted carrots

brussels sprouts with pecorino

teriyaki-roasted broccolini

peas with caramelized shallots

garlic mashed potatoes

easy turkey gravy

chunky cranberry conserve

contents *continue* >>>

mushroom & gruyère
bread pudding

bourbon baked beans

cabbage & sprout slaw

herbed basmati rice

all-star sides

We all tend to think the protein in a meal is the star on the plate, but why can't a wonderful vegetable be the star, paired with a simple roast chicken? Thanksgiving is a classic example of a meal where you really care more about the sides than the main event!

I remember the first time I went to Zuni Café, the iconic San Francisco restaurant founded by the late and much-missed Judy Rodgers. Judy came to sit with us, which was a thrill, and I asked her so many questions. "Why was the chicken so good?" (Salting it in advance was the secret.) And "What are your most popular dishes?" As it turned out, it wasn't just her famous chicken but any entrée paired with the buttermilk mashed potatoes!

For me, sides are never just an afterthought. When I'm planning a menu I look for a balance of textures and a symphony of flavors that play well with each other. It's like an orchestra; if the trumpets are loud, you don't want every other instrument blaring at the same time. I wouldn't serve a green vegetable like Teriyaki-Roasted Broccolini (page 147) with another green vegetable. However, if I put the Garlic Mashed Potatoes (page 151) on the menu, I might serve it with Mustard-Roasted Meatballs (page 102) and something quiet, like plain roasted Brussels sprouts. Each recipe in this chapter has its own unique profile so you can mix and match your way to the perfect menu.

REALLY EASY

roasted asparagus with parmesan panko

SERVES 4 TO 6

In the spring, I serve asparagus with everything, from lamb and chicken to beef or fish. When I'm developing a recipe, the texture is as important to me as the flavor. I love this crunchy Parmesan panko topping with earthy, tender asparagus.

Good olive oil
½ cup panko (Japanese bread flakes)
1 teaspoon grated lemon zest
¼ teaspoon crushed red pepper flakes
Kosher salt and freshly ground black pepper
2 tablespoons plus ¼ cup freshly grated Italian Parmesan cheese, divided
2 pounds thick asparagus, trimmed and peeled (see note)

Remove and discard 1 to 1½ inches from the bottom of each asparagus. With a vegetable peeler, peel the lower third of each stalk, occasionally dipping the peeler in water to clean the blade.

Preheat the oven to 425 degrees.

Heat 2 tablespoons olive oil in a small (8-inch) sauté pan over medium heat. Add the panko and cook for 2 to 3 minutes, stirring constantly, until lightly browned. Transfer to a bowl and stir in the lemon zest, red pepper flakes, ½ teaspoon salt, ¼ teaspoon black pepper, and the 2 tablespoons Parmesan.

Place the asparagus on a sheet pan, drizzle with 2 tablespoons olive oil, and sprinkle with ¾ teaspoon salt and ½ teaspoon black pepper. Roast for 5 to 9 minutes, depending on the thickness of the asparagus, until just tender. Sprinkle with the remaining ¼ cup Parmesan and roast for another minute to melt the cheese.

Sprinkle generously with the Parmesan panko crumbs and serve hot.

SHORTCUT

chipotle maple mashed sweet potatoes

SERVES 4 TO 5

I knew about store-bought mashed white potatoes, but I didn't realize you could buy frozen mashed sweet potatoes too, and I'm so glad I've discovered them. No one will suspect this sweet and spicy dish wasn't made from scratch.

- 2 (18-ounce) bags Trader Joe's frozen mashed sweet potatoes
- ⅔ cup freshly squeezed orange juice (2 oranges)
- 4 ounces European-style unsalted butter, such as Plugrà, diced
- ¼ cup pure maple syrup
- ¼ teaspoon ground chipotle powder
- Kosher salt and freshly ground black pepper

Put the frozen sweet potatoes and orange juice into a medium saucepan set over medium heat. Cover and cook for 10 minutes, stirring occasionally, until smooth.

Add the butter, maple syrup, chipotle powder, 2 teaspoons salt, and 1 teaspoon pepper and cook for 2 minutes, until heated through. Serve hot.

SHORTCUT

sautéed corn with pesto & parmesan

SERVES 6

My friend Debbie Kosofsky calls this Carrie's Corn because her niece Carrie makes it for her. To me, it's the essence of late summer. Corn is best when it's cooked soon after picking, so buy it from a farm stand, if you can. This is beyond delicious, and store-bought pesto makes it fast.

6 tablespoons (¾ stick) unsalted butter

6 cups fresh corn kernels, cut off the cobs (8 to 10 ears; see note)

Kosher salt and freshly ground black pepper

2 tablespoons good store-bought pesto

1½ tablespoons freshly grated Italian Parmesan cheese

Julienned fresh basil leaves, for garnishing

To prep the corn, place a clean kitchen towel over a sheet pan. Cut the base of the corn cob straight across, then stand it on end and cut the kernels off, cutting from top to bottom.

Heat the butter in a large (12-inch) sauté pan over medium heat. Add the corn, 2 teaspoons salt, and 1 teaspoon pepper and sauté over medium-high, stirring occasionally, for 8 to 10 minutes, until the kernels are cooked through but still firm and starting to brown at the edges of the pan. Remove from the heat.

Stir in the pesto and Parmesan until thoroughly incorporated. Sprinkle on the basil and some salt and serve hot or warm.

SHORTCUT

caramelized butternut squash & cranberries

SERVES 6

The hardest part of roasting butternut squash is peeling and cutting the squash! Starting with precut squash from the grocery store is such a time-saver. Adding brown sugar before it goes into the oven makes the edges browned and so flavorful.

2½ pounds precut butternut squash
Good olive oil
¼ cup light brown sugar, lightly packed
2 tablespoons unsalted butter, diced
¼ teaspoon crushed red pepper flakes
Kosher salt and freshly ground black pepper
½ cup dry Marsala wine
½ cup dried cranberries
1 tablespoon syrupy aged balsamic vinegar, such as Villa Manodori (see note)

Preheat the oven to 425 degrees.

If the pieces of butternut squash are large, cut them in 1-inch dice. Place them on a sheet pan with ¼ cup olive oil, the brown sugar, butter, red pepper flakes, 2 teaspoons salt, and 1 teaspoon black pepper. Toss well with your hands and spread out in one layer. Roast for 30 to 35 minutes, tossing occasionally, until the squash is tender and the edges begin to caramelize.

Meanwhile, put the Marsala and cranberries in a glass measuring cup and microwave on high for 2 minutes. When the squash is done, use a slotted spoon to add the cranberries to the squash, discarding the liquid. Drizzle with the vinegar, sprinkle with salt, toss well, and serve hot or warm.

As opposed to regular balsamic vinegar, aged balsamic is thick and syrupy with less acidic bite, making it good to drizzle on finished dishes.

REALLY EASY

maple & balsamic roasted carrots

SERVES 4 TO 6

Carrots are one of the few vegetables that are delicious all year long. I buy the ones with the tops still attached because they're fresher and sweeter. Roasting them with maple syrup and later drizzling them with balsamic vinegar brings out their intrinsic sweetness.

- 1½ pounds thin rainbow carrots with tops, scrubbed
- ½ pound thin orange carrots with tops, scrubbed
- 1 medium red onion, halved and cut into ¼-inch-thick half-rounds, rings separated
- 4 tablespoons (½ stick) unsalted butter, large-diced
- 2 tablespoons pure maple syrup
- Kosher salt and freshly ground black pepper
- 1½ tablespoons syrupy aged balsamic vinegar, such as Villa Manodori

Preheat the oven to 425 degrees.

Trim the tops and bottoms of the carrots, leaving ½ inch of the tops. If any of the carrots are more than ½ inch in diameter at the thickest point, cut them in half lengthwise.

Place all the carrots and the onions on a sheet pan. (Don't crowd them or they will steam rather than roast.) Add the butter, maple syrup, 1 teaspoon salt, and 1 teaspoon pepper. Roast for 5 minutes to melt the butter. Toss with a spatula.

Place the pan back in the oven for 15 to 20 minutes, turning the pan and tossing the vegetables once halfway through, until the carrots are tender when pierced with a fork. Drizzle with the vinegar, sprinkle with salt, and serve hot.

REALLY FAST

brussels sprouts with pecorino

SERVES 4

Once you've tried roasting or sautéing them, you'll never serve mushy Brussels sprouts again. Lots of Pecorino and black pepper give these so much flavor. If you're in a hurry, you can use store-bought sliced sprouts, but if you buy them and slice them yourself in the food processor, it's still incredibly fast and they will have a little more texture.

3 tablespoons unsalted butter

Good olive oil

1 pound Brussels sprouts, trimmed and thinly sliced (see headnote)

Kosher salt and freshly ground black pepper

2 tablespoons freshly grated Italian Pecorino cheese

½ teaspoon grated lemon zest

Heat the butter and 3 tablespoons olive oil in a large (12-inch) sauté pan over medium to medium-high heat until the butter melts. Add the Brussels sprouts, 1½ teaspoons salt, and ¾ teaspoon pepper.

Toss well and sauté for 8 to 10 minutes, stirring occasionally, until the sprouts are tender. Sprinkle with the Pecorino, lemon zest, and salt and serve hot.

SHORTCUT

teriyaki-roasted broccolini

SERVES 4

Broccolini is simply the easiest, most delicious vegetable ever. It's great just roasted with olive oil plus S&P, but when I want something a little different, I add a combination of bottled teriyaki sauce and sesame oil, and it's an over-the-top side dish.

1 pound broccolini or baby broccoli

1 tablespoon toasted sesame oil

½ cup Soy Vay Veri Veri Teriyaki Marinade & Sauce, shaken

1 teaspoon minced garlic

Kosher salt and freshly ground black pepper

1 tablespoon sesame seeds, toasted (see note)

To toast white sesame seeds, put them in a small (8-inch) dry sauté pan and cook over medium-low heat for 5 to 10 minutes, tossing often, until very lightly browned. Transfer to a plate to cool.

Preheat the oven to 400 degrees.

To prep the broccolini, remove and discard the lower third of the stems. If some of the stalks are thicker, cut them in half lengthwise, slicing the stem and pulling the tops apart.

Place the broccolini on a sheet pan. Drizzle with the sesame oil. Combine the teriyaki, garlic, 1 teaspoon salt, and ½ teaspoon pepper in a 1-cup glass measuring cup and pour it over the broccolini. Toss well and spread the broccolini out in one layer.

Roast for 8 to 10 minutes, until the thicker stems are crisp/tender. Transfer to a platter, add the juices from the pan, and sprinkle with the sesame seeds. Serve hot, warm, or at room temperature.

REALLY FAST

peas with caramelized shallots

SERVES 4 TO 6

Peas are one of the few frozen vegetables that are actually very good, often better than most fresh peas, which can be too starchy. I always keep a bag in the freezer so that when I'm in a rush, I can make this side. It goes with almost any chicken, beef, or lamb dish.

Good olive oil
1½ tablespoons unsalted butter
3 large shallots, peeled and sliced into thin rounds
½ teaspoon sugar
1 pound frozen peas
1½ teaspoons chopped fresh tarragon
Kosher salt and freshly ground black pepper

Heat 1½ tablespoons olive oil and the butter in a medium (10-inch) sauté pan over medium heat. When the butter has melted, add the shallots, separating the rings a bit. Sauté the shallots for 8 to 10 minutes, stirring frequently, until they're tender and beginning to brown. Sprinkle on the sugar and continue cooking for about 3 minutes, until they're a deep brown color but not burnt. Transfer half of the shallots to a plate.

Add the peas and ⅓ cup water to the pan, tossing to combine with the shallots. Bring to a simmer over medium heat and cook for 3 minutes, stirring occasionally, until the peas are tender. Stir in the reserved caramelized shallots, the tarragon, 1 teaspoon salt, and ½ teaspoon pepper. Taste for seasonings and serve hot.

SHORTCUT

garlic mashed potatoes

SERVES 6

Compared to making your own mashed potatoes from scratch, this is ridiculously easy. Store-bought mashed potatoes (I prefer Bob Evans) are fine but they're a little bland. I add slowly cooked garlic and lots of seasonings, and no one will ever know you didn't peel and mash the potatoes yourself!

2 (24-ounce) packages Bob Evans Original mashed potatoes
½ cup half-and-half
6 large or 8 small cloves garlic confit plus some of their oil for serving
2 tablespoons unsalted butter
Kosher salt and freshly ground black pepper

Put the potatoes and half-and-half in a medium saucepan and heat over medium-low heat, stirring occasionally, until smooth. Mash the garlic cloves and stir them into the potatoes with the butter, 1 teaspoon salt, and ½ teaspoon pepper. Serve hot, drizzled with 1 tablespoon of the garlic confit oil.

You can cook a large batch of the garlic, set aside to cool, and refrigerate in a sealed container for 2 weeks.

garlic confit

MAKES ABOUT ½ CUP

Approximately 1 cup good olive oil
1 head garlic, separated into cloves and peeled

Put the olive oil and garlic in a small saucepan and bring the oil to a simmer over medium heat. Make sure all the garlic is covered with oil. Lower the heat and cook at a very low simmer (small bubbles coming to the surface) for 20 to 30 minutes, until the garlic is lightly browned and very tender. (I pull the pan halfway off the heat.) Don't hurry it; you want the garlic to cook slowly.

Cool to room temperature, cover with the lid, and refrigerate for up to 2 weeks.

SHORTCUT

easy turkey gravy

SERVES 4 TO 6

Gravy is one of the most stressful parts of a holiday meal to make! First, you have to make it after the turkey comes out of the oven and before you serve dinner, when there is so much going on, and if you're not careful, you can end up with lumpy gravy. Instead, make this early in the day and add some of the strained drippings from the pan once the turkey is done.

Good olive oil

½ cup sliced shallots, halved lengthwise and thinly sliced crosswise (2 large)

2 tablespoons Cognac or brandy

1 (4-inch) sprig fresh thyme

1 (10½-ounce) can Campbell's turkey gravy (see note)

3 tablespoons dry white wine, such as Pinot Grigio

Kosher salt and freshly ground black pepper

½ tablespoon salted or unsalted butter, diced

Turkey pan drippings, strained

Heat 2 tablespoons olive oil in a small (8-inch) sauté pan over medium-low heat. Add the shallots and cook for 5 minutes, until soft but not browned, stirring occasionally. Off the heat, add the Cognac and thyme, then turn the heat to medium-low and cook for 3 minutes. Be careful; it may flame up.

Stir in the gravy, white wine, ½ teaspoon salt, and ¼ teaspoon pepper and simmer for 3 minutes. Discard the thyme, add the butter, and stir until melted. Stir in the turkey drippings, reheat, and serve hot.

I've tried lots of different canned gravies and Campbell's is by far the best!

SHORTCUT

chunky cranberry conserve

SERVES 6

Of course you can make cranberry sauce by washing and picking through a bag of cranberries and cooking them with fruit and nuts. But if you start with a can of whole berry cranberry sauce, you'll have a cranberry conserve that is perfect for Thanksgiving in half the time.

1 (14-ounce) can Ocean Spray whole berry cranberry sauce
½ Granny Smith apple, peeled and grated (see note)
½ teaspoon finely grated orange zest
2 tablespoons freshly squeezed orange juice
¼ cup raisins
¼ cup coarsely chopped pecans

I grate the apple on the large holes of a box grater, as you would grate carrots.

Place the cranberry sauce, apple, orange zest, and orange juice in a small saucepan over medium-low heat. Bring to a boil, cover, lower the heat, and simmer for 15 minutes, stirring occasionally.

Off the heat, add the raisins and pecans. Cool and refrigerate until ready to serve. Serve cold or at room temperature.

SHORTCUT

mushroom & gruyère bread pudding

SERVES 8 TO 10

I was trying to figure out how to simplify making a savory bread pudding and realized that using Pepperidge Farm stuffing mix would eliminate the tedious steps of cutting and toasting all that bread. I use the herb seasoned variety, but you can choose whichever you like. It's the perfect Thanksgiving stand-in for stuffing.

7 tablespoons unsalted butter, divided
1½ cups chopped yellow onion (1 large)
2 teaspoons minced garlic (2 cloves)
12 ounces cremini mushrooms, trimmed, caps sliced ¼-inch thick (see note)
¼ cup cream sherry, such as Harvey's Bristol Cream
2 teaspoons minced fresh rosemary leaves
1 (12-ounce) bag Pepperidge Farm Herb Seasoned Cubed Stuffing
3 cups grated Gruyère cheese (8 to 10 ounces), divided
5 extra-large eggs
2¼ cups half-and-half
1¼ cups chicken stock, such as College Inn
Kosher salt and freshly ground black pepper

Wipe the mushroom caps with a paper towel; don't wash them!

Preheat the oven to 350 degrees. Butter a 9 × 13 × 2-inch baking dish with 1 tablespoon of the butter and set aside.

Melt 4 tablespoons of the butter in a medium (10-inch) sauté pan over medium heat. Add the onions and sauté for 7 minutes, stirring occasionally, until tender. Add the remaining 2 tablespoons of butter, the garlic, and mushrooms and cook for 7 to 8 minutes, stirring occasionally, until the mushrooms start to brown. Add the sherry and rosemary and simmer for 2 minutes.

Meanwhile, put the stuffing mix into a large bowl. Stir in the mushroom mixture and cool for 5 minutes. Stir in 2 cups of the cheese. In a separate bowl, whisk together the eggs, half-and-half, chicken stock, 2 teaspoons salt, and 1 teaspoon pepper. Pour the custard mixture over the crumb mixture and stir well. Set aside for 10 minutes, stirring occasionally, for the crumbs to absorb most of the liquid.

Transfer to the prepared baking dish, smooth the top, and sprinkle evenly with the remaining cup of Gruyère. Bake for 40 to 50 minutes, until the top is golden brown and the custard is set in the center. Serve warm.

SHORTCUT

bourbon baked beans

SERVES 6

You can make baked beans that soak overnight, and then simmer with bacon and maple syrup for 6 hours in the oven. Or you can start with a couple of cans of baked beans and end up with a dish that tastes like it cooked for 6 hours!

¼ pound thick-sliced applewood smoked bacon, 1-inch diced

1 cup chopped yellow onion

Canola or vegetable oil

Two (16-ounce) cans Bush's Best baked beans, such as Maple & Cured Bacon (see note)

⅓ cup store-bought barbecue sauce, such as Stubb's Original

¼ cup ketchup, such as Heinz

¼ cup good maple syrup

2 teaspoons good Dijon mustard, such as Grey Poupon

3 tablespoons mild bourbon, such as Maker's Mark

I use Bush's Best Maple & Cured Bacon Baked Beans, but you can use any Bush's flavor you prefer.

In a small (8 to 9-inch) heavy-bottomed pot or Dutch oven, such as Le Creuset, sauté the bacon over medium heat for 5 minutes, stirring occasionally, until browned and crisp. Transfer the bacon to a plate with a slotted spoon. Add the onions to the pot and sauté for 5 to 7 minutes, stirring occasionally, until starting to brown. (Add a little canola or vegetable oil if the onions are dry.)

Pour the baked beans into the pot and stir in the barbecue sauce, ketchup, maple syrup, and mustard. Off the heat, stir in the bourbon and return the bacon to the pot. Bring to a boil, lower the heat, and simmer uncovered for 15 minutes, stirring occasionally, until thickened. Serve hot.

SHORTCUT

cabbage & sprout slaw

SERVES 6

Coleslaw doesn't get any easier—or more delicious—than this. Every grocery store now sells bags of shredded cabbage and carrots. I've added shredded Brussels sprouts for flavor and texture and it takes no time at all.

1 cup good mayonnaise, such as Hellmann's
3 tablespoons apple cider vinegar
2 tablespoons sugar
2 teaspoons good Dijon mustard, such as Grey Poupon
1 teaspoon celery seeds
1 teaspoon celery salt
Kosher salt and freshly ground black pepper
16 ounces shredded coleslaw mix, preferably with carrots
4 ounces shredded or sliced Brussels sprouts

In a large bowl, whisk together the mayonnaise, vinegar, sugar, mustard, celery seeds, celery salt, 1 teaspoon kosher salt, and ½ teaspoon pepper. Add the coleslaw mix and shredded Brussels sprouts and toss to coat with the dressing. Chill for at least one hour.

Taste for seasonings and serve cold or at room temperature.

ONE POT

herbed basmati rice

SERVES 3 TO 4

I'm obsessed with my rice cooker. There are expensive ones that measure the water for you and inexpensive ones that require you to add the water, but they all result in perfectly cooked rice. Here I've added butter and fresh herbs for the most delicious rice ever.

- 2 cups white basmati rice, such as Texmati
- 2 teaspoons kosher salt
- 3 tablespoons unsalted butter, divided
- 3 tablespoons minced fresh parsley
- 3 tablespoons minced scallions, white and green parts
- 2 tablespoons minced fresh dill

For the rice cooker: Follow the directions on your rice cooker. Place the rice, salt, and 2 tablespoons of the butter (plus 3½ cups water if your rice cooker doesn't have a reservoir for water) in the rice cooker. Press the appropriate settings and let the cooker do the work. When the rice is done, fluff with a fork and stir in the parsley, scallions, dill, and the remaining tablespoon of butter. Serve warm.

For the stovetop: Combine the rice, 3½ cups water, the salt, and 2 tablespoons of the butter in a medium heavy-bottomed saucepan. Bring to a boil over high heat; reduce the heat to low, stir once, and cover tightly. Simmer (I need to pull the pot half off the burner to keep it from boiling over) for 15 minutes, then turn off the heat and allow the rice to sit covered for 5 minutes. Fluff with a fork and stir in the parsley, scallions, and dill. Top with the remaining tablespoon of butter and serve warm.

dessert

fresh peach & almond cake

strawberries romanoff

oranges with whipped yogurt & pistachios

kahlúa egg cream float

cherry clafoutis

strawberry rhubarb compote

strawberry rhubarb eton mess

cherry berry crumble

irish coffee affogato

warm “apple pie” applesauce

candied pecans

raspberry cheesecake

contents *continue* >>>

strawberries with white chocolate

white chocolate bark
with raspberries & pistachios

one-bowl chocolate cupcakes
with vanilla buttercream

chocolate dessert board

simple *is* sophisticated

I want a gorgeous dessert to be the crowning glory of a meal. It's the treat at the end, and I like it to be memorable. When I'm developing a recipe, I decide which ingredient is the star and then add supporting players to make the star shine more brightly. For my Irish Coffee Affogato (page 188), instead of just vanilla ice cream with a shot of espresso, I added Kahlúa, which deepens the coffee flavor, and some Irish whiskey to give it an edge. It still tastes like coffee with vanilla ice cream—but it's the best coffee with vanilla ice cream you've ever had. My One-Bowl Chocolate Cupcakes with Vanilla Buttercream (page 201) have some coffee in the cake because it turns out that coffee makes chocolate taste better, too. The easy vanilla buttercream is—literally—the icing on the cake.

In addition to adding ingredients to make the star taste better, I look for synergy between ingredients. I love the combination of raspberries and cream, so instead of serving a simple cheesecake from a bakery, I make my Raspberry Cheesecake (page 194) with homemade raspberry sauce and fresh berries. The sauce is so easy, and I pour it over the cheesecake and pile it with raspberries. Now you have a real dessert! The creamy vanilla cheesecake makes the sweet raspberry sauce and raspberries taste better and vice versa.

It turns out, as with everything else, a simple dessert done right is actually more sophisticated and appealing than a dessert with too many flavors—and that's exactly what I'm looking for in each recipe.

MAKE AHEAD

fresh peach & almond cake

SERVES 8

I like to make this moist, delicious ricotta cake with whatever fruit is in season, and peaches are especially nice in summer. It's not too sweet, so it's good for brunch or dessert and it always comes out perfectly. I added almond to give the peaches more depth of flavor.

- 10 tablespoons (1¼ sticks) unsalted butter, at room temperature
- 1 cup granulated sugar
- 3 extra-large eggs, at room temperature
- 1 cup fresh whole milk ricotta, at room temperature
- 2 tablespoons sour cream
- 1 teaspoon pure vanilla extract
- ½ teaspoon pure almond extract
- 2 tablespoons almond paste, minced, at room temperature
- 1¼ cups all-purpose flour
- 1 tablespoon baking powder
- 1 teaspoon kosher salt
- 2 small fresh peaches, sliced in ½-inch wedges, plus more wedges for serving
- ¼ cup sliced almonds
- 1 tablespoon turbinado sugar, such as Sugar in the Raw
- Good vanilla ice cream, such as Häagen-Dazs, for serving

Preheat the oven to 375 degrees. Butter and flour a 9-inch round springform pan, tapping out the excess flour.

Place the butter and granulated sugar in the bowl of an electric mixer fitted with the paddle attachment and beat on medium speed for 3 minutes, until light and fluffy, scraping down the bowl with a rubber spatula. With the mixer on medium-low, add the eggs one at a time, scraping down the bowl and mixing until smooth. Add the ricotta, sour cream, vanilla, and almond extract, and mix until combined. Add the almond paste and mix on medium speed until the almond paste is incorporated. Don't worry; you can't overbeat it at this stage.

In a small bowl, combine the flour, baking powder, and salt. With the mixer on low, slowly add the dry ingredients to the batter, mixing just until combined. Pour the batter into the prepared pan and smooth the top. Arrange the peaches in one layer in concentric circles. Sprinkle with the almonds, then the turbinado sugar. Bake for 35 to 45 minutes, until the top is nicely browned and a toothpick inserted in the center comes out clean.

Allow the cake to cool in the pan on a baking rack for 15 to 20 minutes, then transfer to a cake plate. Serve warm with ice cream and a slice of peach on the side.

strawberries romanoff

SERVES 4 TO 5

Strawberries Romanoff is a dessert credited to Auguste Escoffier from the time when he was working in London in the 1920s. When strawberries are in season, this is the most elegant dessert. The sweetness of the strawberries is enhanced with a little sugar, and the Cointreau gives it an appealing citrus edge.

6 cups fresh strawberries, hulled and halved or quartered (about 2 pounds)
⅓ cup Cointreau liqueur or orange juice
¼ cup granulated sugar

FOR THE TOPPING
¾ cup cold heavy cream
½ cup cold sour cream
3 tablespoons light brown sugar (see note)
2 tablespoons confectioners' sugar
1 teaspoon pure vanilla extract
Freshly grated orange zest, for serving

If your brown sugar has hardened, microwave it for one minute.

Place the strawberries in a medium bowl, add the Cointreau and granulated sugar, and toss gently to coat the berries. Cover and refrigerate for at least one hour.

For the topping, in the bowl of an electric mixer fitted with the whisk attachment, combine the heavy cream, sour cream, brown sugar, confectioners' sugar, and vanilla. Beat on medium speed until it forms soft peaks. Refrigerate until ready to serve.

Spoon the strawberries and their juices into 4 or 5 bowls or glasses. Spoon a dollop of the cream mixture on top, sprinkle with a little orange zest, and serve immediately.

MAKE AHEAD: *Prepare the strawberry mixture and the topping and refrigerate them separately for up to 2 hours. Assemble the dessert just before serving.*

oranges with whipped yogurt & pistachios

SERVES 6

My friend Elsa Walsh made this dessert for me when I was visiting her. It's based on a recipe from the wonderful British cookbook writer Diana Henry. You can prepare the fruit and marinate it a few days in advance and then just assemble it with the creamy, sweet whipped yogurt and salty pistachios before serving.

- ⅔ cup freshly squeezed orange juice (2 large)
- ½ cup sugar
- 2 large navel oranges
- 2 large Cara Cara oranges
- 2 large blood oranges
- 1 small pink grapefruit
- Whipped Yogurt, for serving
- Roasted, salted pistachios, coarsely chopped, for serving

Combine the orange juice and sugar in a small saucepan and bring to a boil. Lower the heat and simmer for 15 to 20 minutes, until syrupy but not caramelized.

Meanwhile, cut off both ends from each piece of fruit. Stand each piece on a flat end and run your knife down the side, removing *all* of the peel and white pith. Slice the fruit crosswise ½ inch thick, remove any seeds, and place the slices in a shallow bowl. Pour the orange syrup over the fruit and refrigerate until cold.

To serve, place the fruit and syrup in bowls, top with a dollop of the whipped yogurt, and sprinkle with the salted pistachios. Serve cold.

whipped yogurt

MAKES 2 CUPS

- 1½ cups (12 ounces) 5% plain Greek yogurt, such as Fage
- ⅓ cup cold heavy cream
- 3 tablespoons pure maple syrup
- ¾ teaspoon pure vanilla extract

Put the yogurt, cream, maple syrup, and vanilla in the bowl of an electric mixer fitted with the whisk attachment. Whisk on low speed to combine, then raise the speed to medium-high and whisk until it just forms soft peaks.

MAKE AHEAD: *Prepare the fruit and whipped yogurt and store them separately in the fridge for up to a few days. Assemble and top with pistachios before serving.*

kahlúa egg cream float

SERVES 4

Classically, an egg cream is made by combining chocolate syrup with milk and adding seltzer. Adding Kahlúa makes it a grown-up dessert drink. Egg creams are traditionally made with Fox's U-Bet chocolate syrup, but I prefer Hershey's syrup.

¾ cup Hershey's chocolate syrup, plus more for drizzling

1 cup cold heavy cream

4 tablespoons Kahlúa or other coffee liqueur

Cold San Pellegrino sparkling water (see note)

2 pints good vanilla ice cream, such as Häagen-Dazs

San Pellegrino is preferable to club soda here; its carbonation is softer, it's less salty, and the ice cream will sink with club soda.

For each float, pour 3 tablespoons chocolate syrup, ¼ cup of cream, and 1 tablespoon Kahlúa into a 16-ounce glass. While beating vigorously with a fork, slowly add sparkling water until the glass is ¾ full.

Add 2 scoops of ice cream, then fill the glass with more sparkling water. Drizzle a little syrup on the ice cream. Serve ice cold with a straw and a long-handled spoon.

PREP AHEAD

cherry clafoutis

SERVES 6

Despite its funny name, clafoutis is delicious and as easy to prepare as making pancakes in the morning. The Grand Marnier–flavored batter can be made ahead of time, then poured over the cherries and baked before dinner.

- 1 tablespoon unsalted butter, at room temperature
- 2 tablespoons plus ⅓ cup granulated sugar, divided
- 2 cups frozen sweet cherries, such as Woodstock (12 ounces)
- 2 tablespoons Grand Marnier
- 1½ cups heavy cream
- 3 extra-large eggs
- 6 tablespoons all-purpose flour
- ½ teaspoon baking powder
- 2 teaspoons pure vanilla extract
- ¼ teaspoon kosher salt
- Confectioners' sugar, for sprinkling

Put confectioners' sugar in a small strainer—not over the clafoutis—then lightly tap the side of the strainer over the clafoutis for a light dusting of sugar.

Preheat the oven to 350 degrees. Place a 9 × 1½-inch round gratin dish on a sheet pan lined with parchment paper. Spread the butter over the bottom and sides of the dish. Sprinkle the 2 tablespoons granulated sugar on the bottom and sides.

Distribute the cherries evenly in the dish and drizzle with the Grand Marnier. Place the remaining ⅓ cup granulated sugar, the cream, eggs, flour, baking powder, vanilla, and salt in a blender and blend for one full minute, scraping down the sides, until smooth and frothy. Pour the mixture carefully over the cherries.

Bake for 40 to 45 minutes, until the top is browned and the middle is just set when a knife inserted in the center comes out clean. (If the top is getting very brown, cover loosely with aluminum foil for the last 10 minutes.)

Set aside to cool for 20 minutes. (It will fall as it cools.) Sprinkle with the confectioners' sugar (see note) and serve warm or at room temperature.

MAKE AHEAD

strawberry rhubarb compote

MAKES 3 CUPS

Compotes are generally made by cooking fruit with sugar for a while until the juices thicken. I speed up the process by cooking the fruit for just 10 minutes and adding strawberry jam, which thickens it and also intensifies the strawberry flavor. I serve this warm for dessert with ice cream or as part of an Eton Mess (page 184), but it's also good on waffles, pancakes, or yogurt.

- 1 pound fresh strawberries, hulled and 1-inch diced
- 1 pound fresh rhubarb, trimmed and ¾-inch diced
- ½ cup sugar
- 1 teaspoon freshly grated orange zest
- ⅓ cup freshly squeezed orange juice
- ¼ cup good strawberry preserves, such as Tiptree

Place the strawberries, rhubarb, sugar, orange zest, and orange juice in a medium (10-inch) Dutch oven, such as Le Creuset, and toss well. Bring to a boil, lower the heat, cover, and simmer for 5 minutes. Uncover and cook at a low boil (more than a simmer) for 5 more minutes. Stir in the strawberry jam and set aside to cool. Refrigerate for up to a week. Serve warm, at room temperature, or cold.

SHORTCUT

strawberry rhubarb eton mess

SERVES 6

This is a great way to use Strawberry Rhubarb Compote, layering it in glasses with crushed (store-bought) meringues and whipped cream. The flavor and textures are fantastic! You can buy meringue cookies, shells, or kisses for this; the shape doesn't matter because they will be crumbled anyway.

1½ cups cold heavy cream
⅓ cup sugar
3 tablespoons mascarpone, crème fraîche, or sour cream
1 teaspoon pure vanilla extract
3 cups Strawberry Rhubarb Compote (page 183)
2 to 3 cups very coarsely crushed meringues (about 4 ounces)
Sliced fresh strawberries, for serving

If you overwhip the cream, add a splash of heavy cream and whip it again.

Place the cream, sugar, mascarpone, and vanilla in the bowl of an electric mixer fitted with the whisk attachment and beat on medium speed until the cream forms soft peaks.

Place ¼ cup of the compote in each of six glasses. Add ¼ cup of the meringue and then a generous ¼ cup of the whipped cream, spreading it out. Continue to layer compote, meringue, and whipped cream to almost fill the glasses. Top with a strawberry slice and serve cold.

PREP AHEAD

cherry berry crumble

SERVES 4

Frozen fruit makes a great crumble and you don't even have to worry about what's in season. To prep this ahead, you can make the crumble topping days in advance and refrigerate it. Then it's just assemble, bake, and serve.

- 4 cups frozen mixed berries (20 ounces)
- 1 cup frozen sweet cherries (6 ounces)
- ⅔ cup sugar
- 3 tablespoons cornstarch
- 1 teaspoon freshly grated orange zest
- 2 tablespoons freshly squeezed orange juice
- Oatmeal Crumble
- Good vanilla ice cream, such as Häagen-Dazs, for serving

Preheat the oven to 375 degrees. Space two racks evenly in the oven. Place four (5-inch) ramekins or gratin dishes on two sheet pans lined with parchment paper.

In a large bowl, combine the berries, cherries, sugar, cornstarch, orange zest, and orange juice. Divide evenly among the gratin dishes. Place one cup of the crumble on each dish and bake for 40 minutes, until the juices are bubbling and the crumble is nicely browned. Serve warm with a scoop of ice cream.

oatmeal crumble

MAKES 4 CUPS

- ¾ cup all-purpose flour
- ¾ cup granulated sugar
- ½ cup light brown sugar, lightly packed
- ½ cup quick-cooking rolled oats, such as McCann's
- ¾ teaspoon ground cinnamon
- ¾ teaspoon kosher salt
- ¼ pound (1 stick) cold unsalted butter, small-diced

Place all the ingredients in the bowl of an electric mixer fitted with the paddle attachment and mix on medium-low speed for 3 to 5 minutes, until the mixture is crumbly and not dry. With your hands, form the mixture into big crumbles.

MAKE AHEAD: *Cover and refrigerate the crumble topping for up to a week.*

irish coffee affogato

SERVES 4

This is somewhere between a dessert and a dessert drink, and it's over-the-top delicious. A classic affogato is just hot espresso poured over cold ice cream, but this one is a mash-up of affogato and Irish coffee and takes no time to make.

2 pints good vanilla bean ice cream, such as Häagen-Dazs
4 tablespoons Irish whiskey, such as Jameson
4 tablespoons Kahlúa or other coffee liqueur
8 tablespoons freshly brewed hot espresso (regular or decaf)
1 cup Sweetened Whipped Cream
Milk chocolate or semi-sweet chocolate bar, for garnish (see note)

Soften the ice cream slightly in a microwave to make it just scoopable. Place two scoops of ice cream in each of four low glasses. Pour 1 tablespoon of whiskey and 1 tablespoon of Kahlúa over each serving, then top with 2 tablespoons of hot espresso.

Spoon a dollop of whipped cream on top and use a vegetable peeler to shave some chocolate onto the whipped cream. Serve immediately.

I find softer chocolate such as milk chocolate or semi-sweet easiest to shave. You can microwave harder chocolate for a few seconds to soften it before shaving.

sweetened whipped cream

MAKES 1 CUP

½ cup cold heavy cream
1 tablespoon sugar
¼ teaspoon pure vanilla extract

Pour the cream into the bowl of an electric mixer fitted with the whisk attachment (you can also use a hand mixer or whisk) and beat on low speed for one minute. Add the sugar and vanilla and beat on high until the cream forms soft peaks.

MAKE AHEAD

warm "apple pie" applesauce

SERVES 6 TO 8

Who doesn't love apple pie? But no one loves making pie crust. Instead, I've updated my classic applesauce recipe with apple pie spices and now it's a dessert. All you do is prep the apples and citrus, throw them in a big Dutch oven with sugar, and bake it for an hour and a half. I usually serve it with ice cream, but ginger snaps or vanilla shortbread would be good, too.

- 2 large navel oranges
- 1 large lemon
- 3 pounds Granny Smith apples (6 to 8 apples)
- 3 pounds sweet red apples, such as Macoun or Honeycrisp (6 to 8 apples)
- ¾ cup light brown sugar, packed
- ¼ pound (1 stick) unsalted butter
- 2 teaspoons ground cinnamon
- ½ teaspoon ground nutmeg
- ½ teaspoon ground allspice
- ¼ teaspoon ground cloves
- Good vanilla ice cream, such as Häagen-Dazs, for serving (optional)

An easy way to core an apple is to stand it on end and cut straight down around the core in large chunks.

Preheat the oven to 350 degrees.

With a strip zester, zest the oranges and lemon into a medium (10 to 11-inch) Dutch oven, such as Le Creuset. Juice the oranges and lemon and add to the pot. Peel and core the apples (see note) and toss them in the juice. Add the sugar, butter, cinnamon, nutmeg, allspice, and cloves and stir to coat the apples.

Cover the pot and bake for 1½ hours, or until all the apples are very soft. Use a whisk to break up the apples and stir until chunky/smooth. Serve warm with a scoop of vanilla ice cream, if desired.

MAKE AHEAD

candied pecans

MAKES 6 CUPS

Stephen and Evie McGee Colbert are both from South Carolina. They came to visit and brought me a gorgeous basket of Southern specialties, one of which was Candied Pecans from Meem's Bakery in Douglasville, Georgia. This is my version of those delicious pecans.

1 cup sugar
1 teaspoon ground cinnamon
1 teaspoon kosher salt
1 extra-large egg white
¼ teaspoon pure vanilla extract
1 pound whole pecan halves

Preheat the oven to 275 degrees.

Combine the sugar, cinnamon, and salt in a medium bowl and set aside.

In a large bowl, whisk together the egg white, vanilla, and 1 tablespoon water until frothy and slightly thickened. Add the pecans and toss to coat with the egg white mixture. Add the sugar mixture in thirds and combine well.

Spread the nuts on a sheet pan in one layer and roast for 25 to 35 minutes, tossing every 10 or 15 minutes, until the coating is dried. Set aside to cool completely. Store in sealed containers.

SHORTCUT

raspberry cheesecake

SERVES 6

This is the ultimate "hot-rod" dessert. Making cheesecake is tricky because if it's overbaked even a little, it will crack on top, and if it's underbaked, it will fall in the middle. Instead, I buy a delicious cheesecake from a bakery and add my own topping. All pleasure; no stress.

1 (6-inch) cheesecake from a bakery
2 to 4 half-pints fresh raspberries (12 to 24 ounces)
Fresh Raspberry Sauce

Place the cheesecake on a serving platter. Place the raspberries in a bowl and add enough of the raspberry sauce to coat the berries generously. Toss well.

Spoon the raspberries and sauce on top of the cheesecake, allowing some of the raspberry sauce to drip down the sides. Chill and serve cold or at room temperature.

fresh raspberry sauce

MAKES 2 CUPS

1 half-pint fresh raspberries (6 ounces)
½ cup sugar
1 cup seedless raspberry jam (12 ounces)
1 tablespoon framboise liqueur

Combine the raspberries, sugar, and ¼ cup water in a small saucepan. Bring to a boil, lower the heat, and simmer for 4 minutes. Pour the cooked raspberries, the jam, and framboise into the bowl of a food processor fitted with the steel blade and process until very smooth. Chill until ready to serve.

BARELY COOKING

strawberries with white chocolate

MAKES ABOUT 12

You can often buy chocolate-covered strawberries in a specialty food store or candy shop, but they aren't hard to make at home.

- 1 pint large fresh strawberries (about 12)
- 1 bar good white chocolate, such as Lindt (about 4 ounces)

Line a sheet pan with parchment paper and place a wire rack on top. Arrange the strawberries on the rack, leaving space between them.

Finely chop the white chocolate and place it in a microwave-safe bowl. Microwave on high for 30 seconds, then stir with a rubber spatula. Keep heating and stirring in 30-second intervals until the chocolate is *almost* melted. Stir until smooth.

With a teaspoon, drizzle the chocolate over each strawberry. Allow to set at room temperature and serve. To make ahead, refrigerate for up to a day.

white chocolate bark
with raspberries & pistachios

MAKES 16 PIECES

White chocolate is such a great base for freeze-dried raspberries and salty pistachios. The sweet-and-salty thing is great after dinner with a glass of sweet dessert wine or as part of a dessert board. Freeze-dried raspberries are widely available in stores and online.

16 ounces good white chocolate, finely chopped (see note)
½ cup freeze-dried raspberries, coarsely chopped
½ cup roasted, salted pistachios, coarsely chopped

Be sure to use very good white chocolate (not chips) such as Lindt, Callebaut, or Valrhona.

Using a pencil, draw an 8 × 10-inch rectangle on a piece of parchment paper. Turn the parchment paper over so the pencil mark doesn't get onto the chocolate and place it on a sheet pan.

Place ¾ of the white chocolate in a microwave-safe bowl and microwave on high for 30 seconds. Stir the chocolate with a rubber spatula, return it to the microwave for another 30 seconds, then stir again. Continue to heat and stir in 30-second intervals until the chocolate is *just* melted. Immediately stir in the remaining chocolate and allow it to sit at room temperature, stirring often, until it's completely smooth. (If you need to heat it a little more, place it in the microwave for another 15 seconds.)

Pour the melted chocolate onto the parchment paper and spread it to fill the drawn rectangle. Sprinkle evenly with the raspberries and pistachios and press lightly to set the fruit and nuts in the chocolate. Set aside at room temperature to harden for at least 2 hours, or refrigerate for 20 minutes. Break the bark into pieces and serve at room temperature. The bark can be stored in airtight containers for 2 to 3 weeks.

MAKE AHEAD

one-bowl chocolate cupcakes
with vanilla buttercream

MAKES 16 CUPCAKES

These one-bowl chocolate cupcakes are deeply chocolaty and moist, and the intensity of the vanilla buttercream balances the chocolate perfectly. Make and frost the cupcakes in advance, place them in a sealed container, and refrigerate them for up to a week.

1½ cups all-purpose flour
1½ cups sugar
1 cup unsweetened cocoa powder
1½ teaspoons baking soda
¾ teaspoon baking powder
1 teaspoon kosher salt
2 extra-large eggs, at room temperature
1 cup buttermilk, shaken, at room temperature
½ cup vegetable or canola oil
½ cup sour cream, at room temperature
¼ cup hot brewed coffee
2 teaspoons pure vanilla extract
Easy Vanilla Buttercream (recipe follows)

Preheat the oven to 350 degrees. Brush the tops of two 8-cup muffin pans with oil and line the cups with paper liners.

Sift the flour, sugar, cocoa powder, baking soda, baking powder, and salt into a large bowl. Make a well in the dry ingredients and add the eggs, buttermilk, oil, sour cream, coffee, and vanilla. Stir the mixture with a rubber spatula until smooth.

Scoop the batter into the cupcake liners with a standard (2¼-inch) ice cream scoop. Bake in the center of the oven for 20 to 25 minutes, until a toothpick comes out clean. Cool for 10 minutes, remove from the pans, and allow to cool completely.

Fit a pastry bag with a large star tip and fill the bag halfway with the buttercream frosting. Pipe onto the cupcakes. Serve at room temperature.

recipe continues >>>

easy vanilla buttercream

FROSTS 16 CUPCAKES

8 ounces cream cheese (not whipped), at room temperature

½ pound (2 sticks) unsalted butter, at room temperature

1 teaspoon pure vanilla extract, such as Nielsen-Massey

1 teaspoon pure vanilla bean paste, such as Nielsen-Massey

⅛ teaspoon kosher salt

¾ pound sifted confectioners' sugar

Place the cream cheese and butter in the bowl of an electric mixer fitted with the paddle attachment. Mix on medium-low speed just until smooth. Mix in the vanilla extract, vanilla bean paste, and salt. With the mixer still on medium-low, slowly add the sugar and mix just until combined. (Don't whip it!)

Use immediately or refrigerate and bring back to room temperature before piping.

ASSEMBLED

chocolate dessert board

SERVES 4

I first encountered the concept of a dessert board in the South of France, at a restaurant right on the beach in Cannes. It consisted of all kinds of cakes, tarts, fruit, and chocolate and looked insanely appealing. Since then, it's been my go-to, no-cook solution to dessert for a crowd. For this chocolate dessert board, I collected chocolate cakes, cookies, and bars—anything with chocolate—and assembled them in color blocks on a big wooden board. It may involve no cooking at all, but man, does it look impressive, and everyone gets to choose their favorite treats.

Brownies

White Chocolate Bark with Raspberries & Pistachios (page 198)

Strawberries with White Chocolate (page 197)

Fran's chocolate-covered caramels

Chocolate truffles

Pecan bars with chocolate drizzle

Black & white cookies

Coconut macaroons dipped in chocolate

Oranges dipped in chocolate

Green grapes

breakfast & brunch

lemon blueberry muffins

breakfast panna cotta

carissa's avocado toast

ricotta scrambled eggs

seriously crispy bacon

breakfast deviled eggs

maple irish oatmeal

buttermilk belgian waffles

red berry smoothies

nutella & banana sandwiches

bagels & smoked salmon
with scallion, caper, dill cream cheese

cornmeal pound cake

in praise of brunch

Of all the times I invite people to the house, I think Sunday at noon is my favorite. Everyone has done their chores for the weekend, they've had a nice rest, and they're full of energy. On Saturday, I can shop for ingredients and prep ahead so that on Sunday morning I can wake up, have some coffee and toast, crank up the tunes, and have a wonderful morning cooking brunch for my friends.

But here is the other reason I love to make Sunday brunch: the food is basically breakfast food dressed up for a party. Instead of fancy dishes like eggs Benedict and quiche Lorraine that are so rich you need to take a nap afterwards, I prefer to make breakfast dishes like Bagels & Smoked Salmon with Scallion, Caper, Dill Cream Cheese (page 230) that require virtually no cooking at all. Or I make Buttermilk Belgian Waffles (page 224) with all kinds of toppings like Strawberry Rhubarb Compote (page 183) or fresh berries and maple syrup. If I'm having a crowd, I can make a big batch of Ricotta Scrambled Eggs (page 216), which are no more difficult than making plain scrambled eggs (but so much better!) while a tray of Seriously Crispy Bacon (page 219) roasts in the oven. Who doesn't want scrambled eggs and bacon, not to mention the house smells so good when everyone arrives!

The trick to making a Sunday brunch special is to make it feel like a dinner party—just a little earlier in the day. When guests arrive, I greet them with a drink like Watermelon Lemonade (page 28) or a Kir Royale (Champagne with a splash of framboise). Then we hang out in the living room with appetizers like Breakfast Deviled Eggs (page 220) and Salmon Rillettes (page 43) before we go into the kitchen for the main course.

And what's a meal without dessert? You want something special that's delicious but not as sweet as a chocolate cake. I think toasted Cornmeal Pound Cake (page 233) with a little butter and jam or Breakfast Panna Cotta (page 212) with berries and granola feel like dessert for breakfast, don't you? Everyone goes home feeling happy and satisfied, and you haven't exhausted yourself hosting a dinner party that goes late into the night. All the fun and none of the stress. How great is that??

PREP AHEAD

lemon blueberry muffins

MAKES 16 LARGE MUFFINS

At Barefoot Contessa, we probably sold millions of blueberry muffins. I've updated my original recipe, but the combination of blueberries, vanilla, and lemon is still so good. Paper "tulip" baking liners make them easy to get out of the pan!

3 cups all-purpose flour
1½ cups granulated sugar
4½ teaspoons baking powder
1 teaspoon kosher salt
½ teaspoon baking soda
2 teaspoons finely grated lemon zest
1¼ cups whole milk
2 extra-large eggs
½ pound (2 sticks) unsalted butter, melted and cooled slightly
1 teaspoon pure vanilla extract
2 cups fresh blueberries (12 ounces), stems removed, divided
1 tablespoon turbinado sugar, such as Sugar in the Raw

PREP AHEAD: *Prepare the batter, cover the bowl, and refrigerate for up to one day. Scoop and bake before serving. Cold batter will take an extra 5 minutes to bake.*

Preheat the oven to 400 degrees. Place 16 "tulip" baking liners in two muffin pans.

Sift the flour, granulated sugar, baking powder, salt, and baking soda into a large bowl. Stir in the lemon zest. Make a well in the middle of the mixture.

Whisk the milk and eggs together in a 4-cup glass measuring cup. Slowly whisk in the melted butter and vanilla. Pour the wet ingredients into the middle of the dry ingredients and stir with a rubber spatula just until combined. Fold in 1½ cups of the blueberries.

With a standard (2¼-inch) ice cream scoop, place rounded scoops of batter into the lined muffin cups. Distribute the remaining ½ cup blueberries on top, pressing down slightly. Sprinkle with the turbinado sugar. Bake for 20 to 25 minutes, until a toothpick inserted in the middle of a muffin comes out clean. Serve warm or at room temperature.

MAKE AHEAD

breakfast panna cotta

SERVES 8

My friend Erin French owns The Lost Kitchen in Freedom, Maine. She has written two amazing cookbooks and one of them had a breakfast panna cotta, which I thought was a genius idea! I've dressed up my own panna cotta recipe for breakfast with fruit and granola.

2 teaspoons (1 packet) unflavored gelatin
3 cups heavy cream, divided
2 cups plain whole milk yogurt
2 teaspoons pure vanilla extract
Seeds scraped from 1 vanilla bean
1½ tablespoons pure maple syrup
½ cup sugar
2 cups good granola, such as Bola, for serving
3 cups mixed blueberries, raspberries, and sliced strawberries, for serving

In a small bowl, stir the gelatin into 3 tablespoons of cold water and set aside for 10 minutes.

Meanwhile, in a large bowl, whisk together 1½ cups of the cream, the yogurt, vanilla extract, vanilla seeds, and maple syrup. Heat the remaining 1½ cups of cream and the sugar in a small saucepan and bring to a simmer over medium heat, stirring until the sugar dissolves. Off the heat, add the gelatin to the hot cream, stirring until the gelatin dissolves. Pour the hot cream-gelatin mixture into the cream-yogurt mixture.

Pour carefully into 8 serving glasses (see note) and refrigerate uncovered until cold. When the panna cottas are thoroughly chilled, cover with plastic wrap and chill overnight.

Top each panna cotta with ¼ cup of granola and ⅓ cup of mixed berries and serve cold.

I transfer the panna cotta mixture to a 4-cup glass measuring cup (in batches), which makes it easier to pour into the glasses without leaving drips on the sides.

carissa's avocado toast

SERVES 4

Carissa's is a spectacular bakery in East Hampton. I'd be lost without it. They make seasonal avocado toasts and I particularly like the one made with Meredith Dairy cheese, which is creamy and tangy and delicious with the avocado.

1 lemon
4 ripe Hass avocados, pitted and scooped
¼ teaspoon sriracha
¼ teaspoon crushed red pepper flakes, plus extra for sprinkling
Kosher salt and freshly ground black pepper
4 large slices from a country or sourdough loaf, toasted
2 cubes Meredith Dairy marinated sheep & goat cheese
2 to 3 radishes, thinly sliced
Zest of 1 lemon, for serving

MAKE AHEAD: *Prepare the avocado mixture, cover it with plastic wrap placed directly on the surface, and refrigerate for up to a few hours.*

Juice one of the lemons into a large bowl, discarding the seeds. Add the avocados, mix immediately with the lemon juice, and mash with a dinner fork until almost smooth but still a little chunky. Add the sriracha, red pepper flakes, 1½ teaspoons salt, and ¾ teaspoon black pepper and combine well.

Place the toasted bread on four lunch plates. Spread the avocado mixture generously on the bread. Cut the cheese cubes in half, place a piece in the center of each slice of bread, and artfully arrange some radish slices on the avocado. Sprinkle with red pepper flakes, lemon zest, salt, and pepper and serve at room temperature.

REALLY FAST

ricotta scrambled eggs

SERVES 4

I'm always looking for simple dishes I can make a bit more special for brunch. In this case, I started with scrambled eggs and added ricotta, Parmesan, and chives. No fuss and so delicious!

12 extra-large eggs
½ cup whole milk
Kosher salt and freshly ground black pepper
2 tablespoons unsalted butter
Good olive oil
½ cup fresh whole milk ricotta
4 large slices from a country or sourdough loaf, toasted and buttered
Minced fresh chives, red pepper flakes, and grated Italian Parmesan cheese, for serving

In a medium bowl, whisk together the eggs, milk, 2 teaspoons salt, and 1 teaspoon black pepper.

Heat the butter and 1 tablespoon olive oil in a medium (10-inch) nonstick sauté pan over medium-low heat. Just before the butter is melted, add the eggs and allow them to sit for 30 seconds to cook around the edges. Continue to cook, stirring constantly with a rubber spatula, until they're three-quarters done, or a little custardy. Add the ricotta in dollops and stir it into the eggs (there can be some visible clumps of ricotta), cooking and stirring until the eggs are cooked but still soft.

Place the toast on dinner plates, spoon the eggs onto the toast, and sprinkle with chives, red pepper flakes, Parmesan, and salt. Serve hot.

REALLY EASY

seriously crispy bacon

SERVES 4

Who doesn't want perfectly crisp bacon? The trick in this recipe is dusting the slices with Wondra flour before baking them. Perfectly crisp bacon every time, and no greasy mess on top of the stove.

12 ounces thick-cut applewood smoked bacon (see note)

2 tablespoons Wondra flour

Choose bacon that is cut thicker than the usual grocery store brands, such as Nodine's or D'Artagnan.

Preheat the oven to 400 degrees. Line a sheet pan with aluminum foil.

Arrange the bacon on a board in one layer. Put one tablespoon of the flour in a fine-mesh sieve and dust the bacon lightly and as evenly as possible with the flour. Turn the bacon and dust the other side with one more tablespoon of flour.

Transfer each slice of bacon, shaking off any excess flour, to the prepared sheet pan, placing them very close to each other in one layer. Bake for 12 minutes. With metal tongs, turn each strip of bacon and bake for another 5 to 10 minutes, until nicely browned. Transfer the bacon to a cooling rack. Serve warm or at room temperature.

MAKE AHEAD

breakfast deviled eggs

MAKES 12

Store-bought hard-boiled eggs are a terrific time-saver, but though they are great for egg salad, they tend to be a little tough for deviled eggs. On the other hand, you can make your own hard-boiled eggs days in advance, peel them, and store them in the fridge. This is a fun way to serve bacon and eggs for brunch.

¼ pound sliced bacon

6 hard-boiled eggs, peeled, store-bought or homemade (see note)

Kosher salt and freshly ground black pepper

2½ tablespoons good mayonnaise, such as Hellmann's

1 tablespoon good Dijon mustard, such as Grey Poupon

½ teaspoon sriracha

1 tablespoon minced fresh chives and flake sea salt, for garnish

For hard-boiled eggs, place 6 eggs in a medium saucepan and cover with water. Bring to a simmer and turn off the heat. Allow to sit for 10 minutes. Drain the water and fill the pot with cold tap water. Set aside until the eggs are cool. Crack each egg on the top and bottom, then roll it back and forth on a board, breaking up the shell. Remove and discard the shells.

In a medium (10-inch) sauté pan, cook the bacon over medium heat until crisp. Transfer the bacon to a plate lined with paper towels, reserving the bacon fat. Crumble half the bacon and reserve the rest for another use.

Halve the eggs lengthwise and scoop the yolks into a small bowl. Arrange the egg whites, cut sides up, on a platter and sprinkle them with salt.

Mash the egg yolks with a fork. Add the mayonnaise, mustard, 1 tablespoon of the reserved bacon fat, the sriracha, ¼ teaspoon salt, and ⅛ teaspoon pepper and continue mashing everything together with the fork until thoroughly combined.

Transfer the yolk mixture to a pastry bag fitted with a star tip and pipe into the egg whites. Garnish with the crumbled bacon and sprinkle with the chives, sea salt, and pepper. Serve cold or at room temperature.

maple irish oatmeal

MAKES ONE SERVING

This doesn't even feel like a recipe to me because I make it for breakfast almost every morning. However, I saw that a food website that interviewed me once said "Ina's oatmeal" was their most requested recipe, so here it is. The timing depends on your microwave and your bowl, but once you get it down, you're good forever.

⅓ cup quick-cooking rolled oats, such as McCann's

Kosher salt

Cold whole milk, pure maple syrup, salted butter, and sliced banana, for serving

You can substitute milk for the water if you prefer the oatmeal a little richer.

Place the oats, ½ teaspoon salt, and 1 cup water in a microwave-safe bowl. Microwave on high for 3 to 4 minutes, until thickened. Stir well. Add some cold milk, a drizzle of maple syrup, a pat of butter, and some sliced banana. Serve hot.

PREP AHEAD

buttermilk belgian waffles

MAKES 8 WAFFLES

Belgian waffles are thicker than American waffles and require a Belgian waffle maker. This recipe is from the restaurant Buvette in NYC, where they are served as a waffle sandwich with a fried egg, bacon, and melted Cheddar. It's incredibly decadent and delicious. For brunch, I pair these waffles with berries and maple syrup. You can make the batter up to a day ahead of time and store in the refrigerator.

2 extra-large eggs
1¾ cups buttermilk, shaken
1 teaspoon pure vanilla extract
¼ pound (1 stick) unsalted butter, melted, plus extra for cooking
2 cups all-purpose flour
2 tablespoons granulated sugar
2 teaspoons baking powder
½ teaspoon baking soda
Kosher salt
Toppings such as maple syrup and butter; Strawberry Rhubarb Compote (page 183); or mixed berries with maple syrup and confectioners' sugar

In a large bowl, whisk together the eggs, buttermilk, and vanilla. Slowly whisk in the melted butter. In a small bowl, combine the flour, granulated sugar, baking powder, baking soda, and 2 teaspoons salt. Add the flour mixture to the wet mixture and stir with a rubber spatula until combined. (The batter may be lumpy.) Cover and refrigerate for at least 30 minutes.

Heat a Belgian waffle iron to medium and brush all the surfaces with melted butter. Stir the batter and use ½ cup of batter for each waffle. Cook until very browned and crispy. (Ignore the signal on the waffle maker that indicates it's done!) Cut the waffles apart with a small paring knife and repeat with the remaining batter. Serve hot with your desired toppings.

OZS. 60
50

BARELY COOKING

red berry smoothies

SERVES 2 TO 3

Okay, this isn't exactly rocket science, but it's my favorite smoothie to make. The good news is that I usually have all the ingredients in the house, so I can make it anytime. Everyone loves it.

- 7 ounces 5% plain Greek yogurt such as Fage (about 1 cup)
- ¾ cup freshly squeezed orange juice (2 to 3 oranges)
- 2 cups frozen mixed strawberries and raspberries
- 1 ripe banana, cut in chunks
- 2 tablespoons honey
- ⅛ teaspoon pure vanilla extract

Place all the ingredients in a blender and process for 45 seconds to a minute, until very smooth. Pour into glasses and serve very cold.

nutella & banana sandwiches

MAKES 2 SANDWICHES

My friend Kate Tyler's son, Sam, loves to make these sandwiches for breakfast—or frankly anytime! And he can make them for himself and his sister, Lucy, which is great for Kate. What's not to love?

4 (½-inch-thick) slices challah
1 cup Nutella
1 ripe banana, sliced ¼ inch thick

Lightly toast the challah and, while still warm, spread all four slices thickly with Nutella. Place a single layer of bananas on two of the toasted slices and top with the other two slices, Nutella-side down. Cut in half and serve at room temperature.

PREP AHEAD

bagels & smoked salmon
with scallion, caper, dill cream cheese

SERVES 8

Every other Sunday throughout my childhood, my grandparents would drive from Brooklyn to Connecticut and bring us big bags of bagels, smoked salmon, cream cheese, pastrami, and rye bread as though we didn't have food in Connecticut. I just tweaked the cream cheese with lemon zest, green herbs, and capers. It's really easy and so good.

16 ounces cream cheese, at room temperature
1 teaspoon finely grated lemon zest
2 tablespoons freshly squeezed lemon juice
½ cup minced scallions, white and green parts (3 to 4 scallions)
¼ cup minced fresh dill
2 tablespoons capers in brine, drained
Kosher salt and freshly ground black pepper
4 large everything bagels, halved and toasted
8 ounces thinly sliced smoked salmon, such as Scottish or Norwegian
Thin slices of red onion, capers, and sprigs of dill, for serving

Place the cream cheese, lemon zest, and lemon juice in the bowl of an electric mixer fitted with the paddle attachment and mix on medium speed until smooth. Add the scallions, dill, capers, ½ teaspoon salt, and ¼ teaspoon pepper and mix on low just until combined.

Lay the toasted bagel halves on a board, cut sides up, and spread very generously with the cream cheese mixture. Place one layer of salmon on each half and garnish with red onion slices, capers, and sprigs of dill. Sprinkle with pepper and serve at room temperature.

MAKE AHEAD: *The cream cheese mixture will keep refrigerated for up to 2 days.*

ONE BOWL

cornmeal pound cake

MAKES 1 (9-INCH) LOAF

The New York Times Cooking app is amazing because it has so many delicious and accessible recipes for home cooks. I love both cornbread and pound cake, so I was intrigued by Melissa Clark's mash-up of the two. This is my slight variation on her delicious cake.

- 1 cup sugar
- 1 large lemon
- ½ cup buttermilk, shaken
- 2 extra-large eggs
- 1 teaspoon pure vanilla extract
- ¼ pound (1 stick) unsalted butter, melted and cooled slightly
- ½ cup fine yellow cornmeal, such as Indian Head or Bob's Red Mill
- 1 teaspoon baking powder
- ¼ teaspoon baking soda
- Kosher salt
- 1¼ cups all-purpose flour

Preheat the oven to 350 degrees. Grease and flour a 9-inch loaf pan.

Place the sugar in a large bowl and use a rasp to grate the lemon zest directly into the bowl so you capture the lemon oils. With clean hands, massage the zest and sugar together until combined. Whisk in the buttermilk, eggs, and vanilla, then slowly whisk in the melted butter until smooth. Whisk in the cornmeal, baking powder, baking soda, and 1 teaspoon salt, mixing until smooth. Whisk in the flour just until combined.

Transfer the batter to the prepared pan and bake for 40 to 50 minutes, until the top is golden brown and a toothpick inserted in the center comes out clean. Slice and serve warm or at room temperature.

MAKE AHEAD: *Wrap the cooled cake and refrigerate. To serve, bring to room temperature or slice and toast.*

spring cocktail party

sparkling rhubarb
(page 36)

classic cosmopolitans
(page 32)

roasted shrimp
with lemon caper mayonnaise
(page 39)

salmon rillettes
(page 43)

breakfast deviled eggs
(page 220)

whipped ricotta
with fig jam & grilled bread
(page 47)

one-bowl chocolate cupcakes
with vanilla buttercream
(page 201)

summer lunch

watermelon lemonade
(page 28)

tomato parmesan toasts
(page 67)

chicken souvlaki & tzatziki
(page 101)

fresh peach & almond cake
(page 170)

vanilla ice cream
(purchased)

autumn dinner

champagne or wine

fig, blue cheese & prosciutto tartines
(page 68)

cheese straws
(purchased)

salted cashews
(purchased)

balsamic grilled flank steak
(page 113)

charlie bird's autumn salad
(page 75)

irish coffee affogato
(page 188)

winter brunch

freshly squeezed orange juice

ricotta scrambled eggs
(page 216)

seriously crispy bacon
(page 219)

lemon blueberry muffins
(page 211)

breakfast panna cotta
(page 212)

coffee

PEPIN
ROBUCHON
ULTIMATE VEG
BREAKFAST
WABI-SABI WELCOME
KITCHENS
VIBRANT FOOD
EAT BETTER
SAN FRANCISCO
AMERICAN MASALA
TARTINE
RISE
LA TECHNIQUE
KNOW HOW TO COOK
COOK with JAMIE
MARIO BATALI
NEW YORK CITY Food
MILK STREET
NEW PIE
A Great American Cook
SALT TO TASTE
MARCO CANORA
OPEN KITCHEN
GORDON RAMSAY
GLORIOUS FOOD
Ladies Who Lunch
Ina & Nora Talk Turkey

PORTICO
IRISH BAKERY
FLAVORS of the SUN
HELLEBORES
MEAT
HUCKLEBERRY
Poilâne
FLAVOR
Dessert Person
GATEAU
ROBUCHON
good for you
DINNER SOLVED!
GRAMERCY TAVERN
TWENTY
MARIO BATALI
VANITY FAIR
Ina GARTEN
Ina Garten

resources

Anyone can do something simple. What's hard is to do something that's both simple *and* interesting. These places get it right.

E-E Home, Amagansett, New York. In 2019, Elizabeth Eichner opened her store, E-E Home. Elizabeth had previously been a stylist for Chuck Williams, creating the Williams Sonoma cookbooks, and also styled for Ralph Lauren. When she decided to open a store, she just looked around her house and thought about all the things she already loved. They were all simple products made by artisans from around the world. If you're lucky enough to visit her store, I think you'll be as inspired as I am. Everything is simple and elegant, and because so much of it is handmade, it also has a beating heart. I've loved using her tableware pieces to photograph this book so much that I've ended up buying way too many of them!

Roman & Williams Guild, New York, New York, has been a source of inspiration for me since they opened in 2017. It offers the most extraordinary collection of home goods, including furniture, tableware, linens, and more, all handmade by artisans from all over the world. They are unique and beautiful pieces and I love each one.

Hoare & Hoare Antiques, Bridgehampton, New York, has a collection of charming antiques that give a modern table setting personality and warmth.

LE CREUSET
Baked Beans
Cranberry Sauce

index

Note: Page references in *italics* indicate photographs.

a

Affogato, Irish Coffee, 188, *189*
Almond & Fresh Peach Cake, 170, *171*
Apple(s)
& Butternut Squash Soup, Easy, 56, *57*
Waldorf Salad, 72, *73*
Warm "Apple Pie" Applesauce, 190, *191*
Apricot-Glazed Corned Beef, 106, *107*
Asparagus
Lemon Capellini Primavera, 126, *127*
Roasted, with Parmesan Panko, 134, *135*
Avocado
& Endive Salad, 82, *83*
Toast, Carissa's, 214, *215*

b

Bacon
Breakfast Deviled Eggs, 220, *221*
Frisée aux Lardons, 76, *77*
Seriously Crispy, 218, *219*
Bagels & Smoked Salmon with Scallion, Caper, Dill Cream Cheese, 230, *231*
Balsamic
& Maple Roasted Carrots, 142, *143*
Grilled Flank Steak, 112, *113*
Banana(s)
& Nutella Sandwiches, 228, *229*
Red Berry Smoothies, 226, *227*
Bark, White Chocolate, with Raspberries & Pistachios, 198, *199*
Beans, Bourbon Baked, 158, *159*
Beef
Balsamic Grilled Flank Steak 112, *113*
Corned, Apricot-Glazed, 106, *107*
Skillet Pasta with Sausage & Mozzarella, 122, *123*
Strip Steak with Roquefort Chive Butter, 108, *109*
Berry(ies). ***See also specific berries***
Breakfast Panna Cotta, 212, *213*
Cherry Crumble, 186, *187*
Red, Smoothies, 226, *227*
Blueberry(ies)
Breakfast Panna Cotta, 212, *213*
Lemon Muffins, 210, *211*
Bourbon Baked Beans, 158, *159*
Breads & toasts
Carissa's Avocado Toast, 214, *215*
Fig, Blue Cheese & Prosciutto Tartines, 68, *69*
Mushroom & Gruyère Bread Pudding, 156, *157*
Tomato Parmesan Toasts, 66, *67*
Whipped Ricotta with Fig Jam & Grilled Bread, 46, *47*
Broccolini, Teriyaki-Roasted, 146, *147*
Brussels Sprouts
Cabbage & Sprout Slaw, 160, *161*
with Pecorino, 144, *145*
Buttercream, Easy Vanilla, 202, *203*
Buttermilk Belgian Waffles, 224, *225*

c

Cabbage & Sprout Slaw, 160, *161*
Caipiroska, 34, *35*
Cakes
Cornmeal Pound, 232, *233*
Fresh Peach & Almond, 170, *171*
One-Bowl Chocolate Cupcakes with Vanilla Buttercream, 200, *201*
Caper(s)
& Browned Butter, Roasted Cod with, 116, *117*
Lemon Mayonnaise with Roasted Shrimp, 38, *39*
& Olives, Provençal Chicken with, 96, *97*
Scallion, Dill Cream Cheese, Bagels & Smoked Salmon with, 230, *231*
Carrots, Maple & Balsamic Roasted, 142, *143*
Cauliflower, Roasted, Salad, 84, *85*
Cheese. ***See also* Cream Cheese; Parmesan**
Baked Croque Monsieurs, 78–79, *79*
Blue, Dip, Emergency, 44, *45*
Blue, Fig, & Prosciutto Tartines, 68, *69*
Brussels Sprouts with Pecorino, 144, *145*
Carissa's Avocado Toast, 214, *215*
Cheddar & Chive Omelet, 80, *81*
Crabmeat Gratins, 120, *121*
Fresh Peach & Almond Cake, 170, *171*
Herbed Goat, Spread, 40, *41*
Mediterranean Mezze Board, 48, *48–49*
Mushroom & Gruyère Bread Pudding, 156, *157*
Real Greek Salad, 86, *86–87*
Ricotta Scrambled Eggs, 216, *217*
Skillet Pasta with Sausage & Mozzarella, 122, *123*
Strip Steak with Roquefort Chive Butter, 108, *109*
Waldorf Salad, 72, *73*
Whipped Ricotta with Fig Jam & Grilled Bread, 46, *47*
Cheesecake, Raspberry, 194, *195*
Cherry(ies)
Berry Crumble, 186, *187*
Clafoutis, 180, *181*
Roasted Cauliflower Salad, 84, *85*
Sauce, Roast Duck Legs with, 104, *105*
Chicken
Bowl, Sesame Ginger, 98, *99*
Provençal, with Olives & Capers, 96, *97*
Souvlaki & Tzatziki, 100, *101*
Stock, Homemade, 62, *63*
Tortellini in Brodo, 60, *61*

Chipotle Maple Mashed Sweet Potatoes, 136, 137
Chive(s)
& Cheddar Omelet, 80, 81
Lemon Capellini Primavera, 126, 127
Roquefort Butter, Strip Steak with, 108, 109
Chocolate. *See also* White Chocolate
Cupcakes, One-Bowl, with Vanilla Buttercream, 200, 201
Dessert Board, 204-205, 204-205
Irish Coffee Affogato, 188, 189
Kahlúa Egg Cream Float, 178, 179
Clafoutis, Cherry, 180, 181
Coconut
Frozen Piña Coladas, 30, 31
Cod, Roasted, with Browned Butter & Capers, 116, 117
Coffee, Irish, Affogato, 188, 189
Cointreau
Classic Cosmopolitans, 32, 33
Strawberries Romanoff, 172, 173
Corn
Sautéed, with Pesto & Parmesan, 138, 139
Sweet, Orecchiette with, 124, 125
Cornmeal Pound Cake, 232, 233
Cosmopolitans, Classic, 32, 33
Crabmeat Gratins, 120, 121
Cranberry(ies)
& Caramelized Butternut Squash, 140, 141
Classic Cosmopolitans, 32, 33
Conserve, Chunky, 154, 155
Cream, Sweetened Whipped, 188, 188
Cream Cheese
Easy Vanilla Buttercream, 202, 203
Scallion, Dill, Caper, Bagels & Smoked Salmon with, 230, 231
Croque Monsieurs, Baked, 78-79, 79
Cucumbers
Mediterranean Mezze Board, 48, 48-49
Real Greek Salad, 86, 86–87
Sesame Ginger Chicken Bowl, 98, 99
Cupcakes, One-Bowl Chocolate, with Vanilla Buttercream, 200, 201

d

Dill
Herbed Basmati Rice, 162, 163
Lemon Capellini Primavera, 126, 127
Scallion, Caper Cream Cheese, Bagels & Smoked Salmon with, 230, 231
Dip, Emergency Blue Cheese, 44, 45
Duck Legs, Roast, with Cherry Sauce, 104, 105

e

Egg Cream Float, Kahlúa, 178, 179
Egg(s)
Breakfast Deviled, 220, 221
Cheddar & Chive Omelet, 80, 81
Frisée aux Lardons, 76, 77
Jammy, 76, 77
Ricotta Scrambled, 216, 217
Salad, Truffled, 70, 71
Endive & Avocado Salad, 82, 83
Eton Mess, Strawberry Rhubarb, 184, 185

f

Farro
Charlie Bird's Autumn Salad, 74, 75
Fig(s)
Blue Cheese, & Prosciutto Tartines, 68, 69
Jam & Grilled Bread, Whipped Ricotta with, 46, 47
Fish
Bagels & Smoked Salmon with Scallion, Caper, Dill Cream Cheese, 230, 231
Roasted Cod with Browned Butter & Capers, 116, 117
Roasted Halibut with Potato Chip Crust, 118, 119
Salmon Rillettes, 42, 43
Frico Crisps, 58, 59
Frisée aux Lardons, 76, 77
Fruits. *See specific fruits*

g

Garlic
Confit, 151, 151
Mashed Potatoes, 150, 151
Ginger Sesame Chicken Bowl, 98, 99
Gratin, Crabmeat, 120, 121
Gravy, Easy Turkey, 152, 153

h

Halibut, Roasted, with Potato Chip Crust, 118, 119
Ham
Baked Croque Monsieurs, 78-79, 79
Fig, Blue Cheese & Prosciutto Tartines, 68, 69
Herbs. *See also specific herbs*
Charlie Bird's Autumn Salad, 74, 75
Herbed Basmati Rice, 162, 163
Herbed Goat Cheese Spread, 40, 41

i

Ice cream
Irish Coffee Affogato, 188, 189
Kahlúa Egg Cream Float, 178, 179

k

Kahlúa
Egg Cream Float, 178, 179
Irish Coffee Affogato, 188, 189

l

Leek and Mashed Potato Soup, 64, 65
Lemon
Blueberry Muffins, 210, 211

Capellini Primavera, 126, 127
Caper Mayonnaise with Roasted Shrimp, 38, 39
Watermelon Lemonade, 28, 29
Lentils & French Sausage, 110, 111
Lime
Caipiroska, 34, 35
Lobster Bake, Easy, 114, 115

m

Maple
& Balsamic Roasted Carrots, 142, 143
Chipotle Mashed Sweet Potatoes, 136, 137
Irish Oatmeal, 222, 223
Mayonnaise, Lemon Caper, with Roasted Shrimp, 38, 39
Meat. *See* Beef; Pork
Meatballs, Mustard-Roasted, 102, 103
Mezze Board, Mediterranean, 48, 48-49
Muffins, Lemon Blueberry, 210, 211
Mushroom & Gruyère Bread Pudding, 156, 157
Mustard-Roasted Meatballs, 102, 103

n

Nutella & Banana Sandwiches, 228, 229
Nuts. *See* Almond; Pecans; Pistachios

o

Oats
Maple Irish Oatmeal, 222, 223
Oatmeal Crumble, 186, 187
Olives
& Capers, Provençal Chicken with, 96, 97
Mediterranean Mezze Board, 48, 48-49
Real Greek Salad, 86, 86-87
Omelet, Cheddar & Chive, 80, 81
Oranges
Chipotle Maple Mashed Sweet Potatoes, 136, 137
Red Berry Smoothies, 226, 227
Warm "Apple Pie" Applesauce, 190, 191
with Whipped Yogurt & Pistachios, 174, 175, 176-177

p

Panna Cotta, Breakfast, 212, 213
Parmesan
Charlie Bird's Autumn Salad, 74, 75
Endive & Avocado Salad, 82, 83
Frico Crisps, 58, 59
Mustard-Roasted Meatballs, 102, 103
Panko, Roasted Asparagus with, 134, 135
& Pesto, Sautéed Corn with, 138, 139
Roasted Cauliflower Salad, 84, 85
Skillet Pasta with Sausage & Mozzarella, 122, 123
Tomato Toasts, 66, 67
Pasta
Lemon Capellini Primavera, 126, 127
Orecchiette with Sweet Corn, 124, 125
Skillet, with Sausage & Mozzarella, 122, 123
Tortellini in Brodo, 60, 61
Peach, Fresh, & Almond Cake, 170, 171
Peas
with Caramelized Shallots, 148, 149
Lemon Capellini Primavera, 126, 127
Pecans
Candied, 192, 193
Chunky Cranberry Conserve, 154, 155
Waldorf Salad, 72, 73
Peppers
Chicken Souvlaki & Tzatziki, 100, 101
Real Greek Salad, 86, 86-87
Pesto
Orecchiette with Sweet Corn, 124, 125
& Parmesan, Sautéed Corn with, 138, 139
Tomato Parmesan Toasts, 66, 67
Piña Coladas, Frozen, 30, 31
Pineapple
Frozen Piña Coladas, 30, 31
Pistachios
Charlie Bird's Autumn Salad, 74, 75
& Raspberries, White Chocolate Bark with, 198, 199
& Whipped Yogurt, Oranges with, 174, 175, 176-177
Pork. *See also* Bacon; Ham; Sausage
Mustard-Roasted Meatballs, 102, 103
Potato Chip Crust, Roasted Halibut with, 118, 119
Potato(es)
Garlic Mashed, 150, 151
Mashed, & Leek Soup, 64, 65
Sweet, Chipotle Maple Mashed, 136, 137
Prosciutto, Fig & Blue Cheese Tartines, 68, 69
Pudding, Mushroom & Gruyère Bread, 156, 157

r

Radishes
Carissa's Avocado Toast, 214, 215
Charlie Bird's Autumn Salad, 74, 75
Raisins
Chunky Cranberry Conserve, 154, 155
Waldorf Salad, 72, 73
Raspberry(ies)
Breakfast Panna Cotta, 212, 213
Cheesecake, 194, 195
& Pistachios, White Chocolate Bark with, 198, 199
Red Berry Smoothies, 226, 227
Sauce, Fresh, 194, 195
Rhubarb
Sparkling, 36, 37

Rhubarb *continued*
Strawberry Compote, 182, 183
Strawberry Eton Mess, 184, 185
Rice
Herbed Basmati, 162, 163
Sesame Ginger Chicken Bowl, 98, 99
Rum
Frozen Piña Coladas, 30, 31

s

Salads
Charlie Bird's Autumn, 74, 75
Endive & Avocado, 82, 83
Frisée aux Lardons, 76, 77
Real Greek, 86, 86–87
Roasted Cauliflower, 84, 85
Truffled Egg, 70, 71
Waldorf, 72, 73
Salmon
Rillettes, 42, 43
Smoked, & Bagels with Scallion, Caper, Dill Cream Cheese, 230, 231
Sandwiches
Baked Croque Monsieurs, 78-79, 79
Nutella & Banana, 228, 229
Truffled Egg Salad, 70, 71
Sauce, Fresh Raspberry, 194, 195
Sausage
French, & Lentils, 110, 111
& Mozzarella, Skillet Pasta with, 122, 123
Mustard-Roasted Meatballs, 102, 103
Scallion(s)
Caper, Dill Cream Cheese, Bagels & Smoked Salmon with, 230, 231
Herbed Basmati Rice, 162, 163
Sesame
Ginger Chicken Bowl, 98, 99
Teriyaki-Roasted Broccolini, 146, 147
Shallots, Caramelized, Peas with, 148, 149
Shellfish
Crabmeat Gratins, 120, 121
Easy Lobster Bake, 114, 115
Roasted Shrimp with Lemon Caper Mayonnaise, 38, 39
Shrimp, Roasted, with Lemon Caper Mayonnaise, 38, 39
Slaw, Cabbage & Sprout, 160, 161
Smoothies, Red Berry, 226, 227
Soups
Butternut Squash & Apple, Easy, 56, 57
Mashed Potato & Leek, 64, 65
Tortellini in Brodo, 60, 61
Souvlaki, Chicken, & Tzatziki, 100, 101
Spreads
Herbed Goat Cheese, 40, 41
Salmon Rillettes, 42, 43
Squash
Butternut, & Apple Soup, Easy, 56, 57
Caramelized Butternut, & Cranberries, 140, 141
Charlie Bird's Autumn Salad, 74, 75
Chicken Souvlaki & Tzatziki, 100, 101
Stock, Homemade Chicken, 62, 63
Strawberry(ies)
Breakfast Panna Cotta, 212, 213
Red Berry Smoothies, 226, 227
Rhubarb Compote, 182, 183
Rhubarb Eton Mess, 184, 185
Romanoff, 172, 173
Watermelon Lemonade, 28, 29
with White Chocolate, 196, 197
Sweet Potatoes, Chipotle Maple Mashed, 136, 137

t

Tartines, Fig, Blue Cheese & Prosciutto, 68, 69
Teriyaki-Roasted Broccolini, 146, 147
Tomatoes
Charlie Bird's Autumn Salad, 74, 75
Mediterranean Mezze Board, 48, 48-49
Real Greek Salad, 86, 86–87
Tortellini in Brodo, 60, 61
Truffled Egg Salad, 70, 71
Turkey Gravy, Easy, 152, 153
Tzatziki, Chicken Souvlaki &, 100, 101

v

Vanilla Buttercream, Easy, 202, 203
Vegetables. *See specific vegetables*
Vodka
Caipiroska, 34, 35
Classic Cosmopolitans, 32, 33

w

Waffles, Buttermilk Belgian, 224, 225
Waldorf Salad, 72, 73
Watermelon Lemonade, 28, 29
Whipped Cream, Sweetened, 188, 188
Whiskey
Irish Coffee Affogato, 188, 189
White Chocolate
Bark with Raspberries & Pistachios, 198, 199
Strawberries with, 196, 197

y

Yogurt
Breakfast Panna Cotta, 212, 213
Red Berry Smoothies, 226, 227
Whipped, & Pistachios, Oranges with, 174, 175, 176-177

z

Zucchini
Chicken Souvlaki & Tzatziki, 100, 101

recipe index

drinks & appetizers

Caipiroska, 35
Classic Cosmopolitans, 32
Emergency Blue Cheese Dip, 44
Frozen Piña Coladas, 31
Herbed Goat Cheese Spread, 40
Mediterranean Mezze Board, 48
Roasted Shrimp with Lemon Caper Mayonnaise, 39
Salmon Rillettes, 43
Sparkling Rhubarb, 36
Watermelon Lemonade, 28
Whipped Ricotta with Fig Jam & Grilled Bread, 47

lunch

Baked Croque Monsieurs, 79
Charlie Bird's Autumn Salad, 75
Cheddar & Chive Omelet, 80
Easy Butternut Squash & Apple Soup, 57
Endive & Avocado Salad, 83
Fig, Blue Cheese & Prosciutto Tartines, 68
Frico Crisps, 58
Frisée aux Lardons, 76
Homemade Chicken Stock, 63
Mashed Potato & Leek Soup, 64
Real Greek Salad, 86
Roasted Cauliflower Salad, 84
Tomato Parmesan Toasts, 67
Tortellini in Brodo, 61
Truffled Egg Salad, 71
Waldorf Salad, 72

dinner

Apricot-Glazed Corned Beef, 106
Balsamic Grilled Flank Steak, 113
Chicken Souvlaki & Tzatziki, 101
Crabmeat Gratins, 120
Easy Lobster Bake, 115
French Sausage & Lentils, 110
Lemon Capellini Primavera, 127
Mustard-Roasted Meatballs, 102
Orecchiette with Sweet Corn, 124
Provençal Chicken with Olives & Capers, 97
Roast Duck Legs with Cherry Sauce, 105
Roasted Cod with Browned Butter & Capers, 116
Roasted Halibut with Potato Chip Crust, 119
Sesame Ginger Chicken Bowl, 98
Skillet Pasta with Sausage & Mozzarella, 123
Strip Steak with Roquefort Chive Butter, 109

sides

Bourbon Baked Beans, 159
Brussels Sprouts with Pecorino, 144
Cabbage & Sprout Slaw, 160
Caramelized Butternut Squash & Cranberries, 140
Chipotle Maple Mashed Sweet Potatoes, 136
Chunky Cranberry Conserve, 155
Easy Turkey Gravy, 152
Garlic Mashed Potatoes, 151
Herbed Basmati Rice, 163
Maple & Balsamic Roasted Carrots, 143
Mushroom & Gruyère Bread Pudding, 156
Peas with Caramelized Shallots, 148
Roasted Asparagus with Parmesan Panko, 135
Sautéed Corn with Pesto & Parmesan, 139
Teriyaki-Roasted Broccolini, 147

desserts

Candied Pecans, 193
Cherry Berry Crumble, 187
Cherry Clafoutis, 180
Chocolate Dessert Board, 204
Fresh Peach & Almond Cake, 170
Irish Coffee Affogato, 188
Kahlúa Egg Cream Float, 179
One-Bowl Chocolate Cupcakes with Vanilla Buttercream, 201
Oranges with Whipped Yogurt & Pistachios, 175
Raspberry Cheesecake, 194
Strawberries Romanoff, 172
Strawberries with White Chocolate, 197
Strawberry Rhubarb Compote, 183
Strawberry Rhubarb Eton Mess, 184
Warm "Apple Pie" Applesauce, 191
White Chocolate Bark with Raspberries & Pistachios, 198

breakfast & brunch

Bagels & Smoked Salmon with Scallion, Caper, Dill Cream Cheese, 230
Breakfast Deviled Eggs, 220
Breakfast Panna Cotta, 212
Buttermilk Belgian Waffles, 224
Carissa's Avocado Toast, 215
Cornmeal Pound Cake, 233
Lemon Blueberry Muffins, 211
Maple Irish Oatmeal, 223
Nutella & Banana Sandwiches, 229
Red Berry Smoothies, 227
Ricotta Scrambled Eggs, 216
Seriously Crispy Bacon, 219